U1005682

【实用中文交际指南】

MANNERS MATTER

By Yu Chenggong（余成功 著）

A Practical Guide to Socializing with Chinese

彬彬有礼

SinolinguA
华语教学出版社

First Edition 2018

ISBN 978-7-5138-1577-2
Copyright 2018 by Sinolingua Co., Ltd
Published by Sinolingua Co., Ltd
24 Baiwanzhuang Road, Beijing 100037, China
Tel: (86) 10-68320585 68997826
Fax: (86) 10-68997826 68326333
http://www.sinolingua.com.cn
E-mail: hyjx@sinolingua.com.cn
Facebook: www.facebook.com/sinolingua
Printed by Beijing Xicheng Printing Co., Ltd

Printed in the People's Republic of China

PREFACE

China is known as a land of courtesy and propriety. Propriety (*li*) permeates all aspects of traditional society. Rules of propriety are observed on all occasions such as travelling, sitting, sleeping, banqueting, wedding, funeral, birthday, worship and sacrificial ceremonies, and so on. The two major components of propriety are the spirit and principles of etiquette as well as decorum. The spirit of Chinese etiquette involves exercising filial piety, caring for one's families and being kind and compassionate to others. The principle of decorum is to be humble and respect other people. When interacting with others, one should put down their pride, be humble and show respect to others in order to gain their respect.

Instead of following the Western concept of equality, the Chinese pay much attention to people's social status, roles in relationships and age, which help them determine the identities they should adopt while interacting with others. They consciously speak and behave according to their identities. Someone who is older and has a higher rank can intentionally lower his/her social status through behaviours to appear friendly. On the other hand, it would be inappropriate and impolite for someone who is younger and has a lower rank to speak and behave beyond his/her role.

This book consists of two sections. In Section I "Speaking with Manners", 40 scenarios are carefully selected. They include welcomes and send-offs, forms of address and greetings, dining and seating arrangements, holding and using chopsticks, and so on. There are three reasons for selecting these scenarios. First, they embody protocols still commonly observed in the daily lives of the Chinese people. Second, they involve expressions typical of such settings. Third, both the linguistic expressions and the protocols have distinctive Chinese characteristics. In Section II "Acting with Manners", ten scenarios which have rich Chinese cultural connotations but do not involve direct dialogues are carefully selected with explanations of the protocols behind them, so as to help readers cope with similar situations properly.

The book provides standard and idiomatic expressions suitable for use in these scenarios. To help readers better understand the contexts of use, the expressions are labelled with stars to denote the etiquette indexes. For example, expressions with an average degree of formalness are labelled with three stars, expressions for use in more formal situations are labelled with four or five stars while expressions for casual and informal occasions are labelled with two or one star(s). Expressions with three stars correspond to the content taught in elementary Chinese. Expressions with two or four stars are usually taught at the intermediate level while expressions with one or five star(s) are often taught at the advanced level. At the same time, the classification corresponds to the difference between oral and written languages, for example, expressions with four or five stars tend to be used in written language while those with one or two star(s) tend to be used in oral language. In addition, unconventional or inappropriate expressions are denoted with ● as a reminder for learners to use with caution.

Each scenario in the book comes with expressive and humorous Chinese-style illustrations which vividly explain the relevant protocols and expressions. The tasteful illustrations themselves will also bring certain aesthetic pleasure for foreign readers.

This book is suitable for Chinese language learners of all levels as well as descendants of Chinese immigrants who wish to learn about and pass on Chinese protocols. It is especially useful for foreign readers who wish to understand Chinese social etiquette as part of their work requirements. This book can also serve as a valuable reference material for Chinese language teachers.

I would like to thank all my colleagues at the UWA Confucius Institute for their support. I would also like to thank David Ambrose, former Director of the UWA Confucius Institute for writing the Foreword and Miss Hon Shuzhen from Singapore for the translation. My heartfelt thanks go to Ms Anita, a respectful and amiable senior who promoted Chinese teaching in Western Australia; to Mr Xiao Ye, a Chinese painter living in Western Australia, for his invaluable inspiration; and to both Professor Fan Hong, former Director of the UWA Confucius Institute, and Xiang Yixiao, former Director of Adelaide Confucius Institute, for their great encouragement. My special thanks go to Professor Geng

Hu, Deputy Director of South Base for International Promotion of Chinese at Xiamen University, for his precise guidance and valuable recommendation.

前　言

中国素有“礼仪之邦”之称，“礼”在社会中无时不在，出行有礼，坐卧有礼，宴饮有礼，婚丧有礼，寿诞有礼，祭祀有礼，等等。这里的“礼”包含了礼制精神与礼仪行为两大部分。中国人的礼制精神是亲亲爱人，礼仪原则是自卑尊人。在与人交往时要放低姿态，谦恭待人，尊重他人，以赢得他人的尊重。

跟西方平等的人际观念不太一样，中国人非常在意彼此间的地位、关系、年龄等差距，并以此决定自己以什么礼节来进行交往，尽量让言行都符合自己的身份。当然，职位高、年龄大的一方有意降低自己的身份，会显得具有亲和力；相反的一方却不宜超越自己的身份说话行事，否则就可能不得体、不礼貌。

本书分为两个部分。第一部分“说得有礼”精选了 40 个交际场景，如迎来送往、称呼寒暄、就座用餐、拿用筷子等。选择这些场景，首先是因为它们体现了中国人最常用的交往礼节；其次，它们包含了中国人常用的相关语言表达；再次，不论是礼节本身还是语言表达，都体现着鲜明的中国特色。第二部分“做得有礼”则精选了10个富于中国文化内涵但不直接产生对话的场景，解释了其中蕴含的礼节文化，以帮助读者恰当、得体地应对类似情境。

本书为这些交际场景配备了标准地道的表达法。为帮助读者更清楚它们的使用语境，本书特意为其标注了相应的礼仪指数。即：以一般正式程度三星为准，更正式的依次为四星、五星，更随意的依次为二星、一星。三星的语言与初级汉语所教内容相当，四星、二星的和中级水平类似，五星、一星的和高级水平类似。同时，这种分级正好和中文书面语与口语的差别对应起来，四星、五星更趋向书面语，而二星、一星更趋向口语。此外，特意用●标出了那些不合习惯或不得体的表达法，以提醒学习者谨慎使用。

同时，本书为每个场景配备了生动诙谐、富有中国风格的插图。这些插图不但形象地阐释了相关礼节、表达法，而且也给读者带来一定的艺术享受。

本书适合由低到高各种程度的中文学习者，也适合希望学习传承中华礼仪的华人移民后代，同时非常适合因工作需要而希望了解中国交际礼仪的母语非汉语读者，并且对从事汉语教学的教师也具有较高的参考价值。

感谢西澳大学孔子学院所有同事们的支持，感谢前任外方院长 David Ambrose 副教授为本书作序，感谢新加坡韩淑珍小姐的翻译；衷心感谢并深深缅怀西澳中文教育事业的前辈 Anita 老师，衷心感谢西澳华人画家小叶老师的可贵启发，以及西澳大学孔子学院前任外方院长凡红教授和阿德莱德孔子学院前任中方院长相沂晓老师的热情鼓励；特别感谢厦门大学汉语国际推广南方基地副主任耿虎教授的精当指导和宝贵推荐。

FOREWORD

Yu Chenggong, or Mike Yu, has not been idle while teaching Chinese to Australian students at the University of Western Australia's Confucius Institute. True to his profession as a teacher, he has seen a need to clarify the social and cultural practices of Chinese people which differ from Western social etiquette, and which often puzzle or embarrass Westerners by the uncertainty of what to do and what not to do in everyday situations when socializing with Chinese people.

This bilingual book is a practical guide to appropriate behaviour and seeks to address and assist learners with the language and behaviour for appropriate conduct in ordinary social intercourse from table manners to gift-giving to funeral condolences.

Language and societies evolve and new locutions enter everyday speech, often to the bewilderment of older generations, but the basic norms of human behaviour in organized society remain fairly constant — dining, hospitality, friendships, births, deaths and marriages, all of which are covered in Yu Chenggong's book.

Mike Yu's Chinese given name, Chenggong, means success. While no guarantee, it is a happy omen for a work which deserves success and should win for its author the gratitude of many foreign students of Chinese.

David Ambrose

Former Director, UWA Confucius Institute

序　言

在西澳大学孔子学院教授中文期间，余成功老师没有让自己闲下来。作为一名专业的中文教师，他看到中国人的社会和文化习俗与西方有着很大的不同，而这些不同之处经常困扰着西方人，甚至在和中国人打交道时常常不知道该做什么、不该做什么。

这本中英双语交际实用指南旨在指导中文学习者在与中国人的日常交往中得体地进行交际。书中涵盖了从餐桌礼仪到送礼以至丧事的诸多社交场景。无论从语言表达或礼节知识上，本书都能给学习者以非常实用的指导。

社会和语言总是在发展变化，新词语也不断涌现，虽然这给老一代人带来一定的困扰，但是基本的社会规范如饮食、待客、交友、出生、婚丧嫁娶等方面相对稳定，而这些社交主题都涵盖在余老师的这本书里面。

余老师的名字“成功”意思是获得预期的美好结果，虽然我不敢说这本书一定会成功，但这至少是一个好彩头，我相信国外众多中文学习者会因读了这本实用指南而向作者表达感激之情。

西澳大学孔子学院前任外方院长 安道卫

目　录
Contents

ONE

SPEAKING WITH MANNERS

The concept of Chinese etiquette, when reflected in language, is demonstrated through many polite words and expressions. The first category are terms of respect, which are used to address others according to the principle of respecting others. Commonly used honorific terms include “qǐng (please), nín (you), guì (you, your), wèi (classifier for people)”, and so on. The second category is written style or elegant wording which is used to stand out from informal verbal language to show respect. Commonly used terms include “fùqin (father), mǔqin (mother), fūren (madam/wife), tàitai (madam/wife), bǎozhòng (take care)", and so on. The third category are humble words which are meant to elevate the status of others through behaving in a humble or even self-deprecating manner. This practice reflects the principle of being modest. Commonly used terms include "nǎli nǎli (by no means), guòjiǎng (I'm flattered), bù gǎn dāng (you flatter me)", and so on. You will come across as formal and polite if you use any of the above categories of expressions, in particular the first and the second categories.

In addition, you may use "yìdiǎnr (a bit)" and "yǒu diǎnr (is a little)" to lessen the intensity and soften the tone in order to sound friendly and self-effacing.

说得有礼

中国文化中的礼仪观念反映在语言上，就会出现很多礼貌性的词语和表达法。具体表现为：一是敬辞，用敬辞来指称对方，体现了尊敬他人的礼仪原则，常用的如“请、您、贵、位”等；二是书面语或雅词。用这种方式来区别开较不正式的口语，以表示尊敬，常用的如“父亲、母亲、夫人、太太、保重”等；三是谦辞，用谦虚甚至贬低自己的方式来提升对方，体现了自卑的礼仪原则，常用的如“哪里哪里、过奖、不敢当”等。说话时用了以上任一方式，尤其是第一或第二种，都可以显得正式而有礼貌。

此外，还可以用“一点儿”和“有点儿”来弱化程度和语气，从而显得友好、低调。

01 How to ask for someone's name
怎么问姓名

When Chinese people meet for the first time, generally they won't ask for the full name. One reason for this is that it may be presumptuous to do so, the other is that it is improper to address a person by their full name or given name even if you know it. People, therefore, generally just ask for the surname when meeting for the first time, as it is very convenient to address people by "surname + title" if you are already aware of his/her position, occupation or academic title.

初次见面时中国人常常不问对方的全名，一个原因是问全名可能显得冒昧，再一个原因就是即便知道了全名，也不太可能用全名或名字来称呼对方，所以一般只问姓。再知道对方的职位、职业或者学位等头衔后，用“姓 + 头衔”来称呼就显得礼貌得体了。

Nǐ xìng shénme ?
你 姓 什 么？

★★ *What is your family name?*

Qǐngwèn , Nǐ jiào shénme míngzi ?
请 问 ， 你 叫 什 么 名 字？

★★★ *Excuse me, what is your name?*

Nín guìxìng ?
您 贵 姓？

★★★★ *What is your surname please?*

Qǐngwèn , nín guìxìng ?
请 问 ， 您 贵 姓？

★★★★★ *Excuse me, what is your surname?*

Qǐngwèn , zěnme chēnghu nín ?
请 问 ， 怎 么 称 呼 您？

★★★★★ *Excuse me, how may I address you?*

Nǐ de míngzi shì shénme ?
● 你 的 名 字 是 什 么？

What is your name?

02 How to address someone you first meet
怎么称呼初次见面的人

When things are not called by their proper names, one's argument cannot stand to reason. Forms of address reflect the various relationships between people, so appropriate forms of address play a very important role in the interaction amongst Chinese people, while inappropriate forms of address may hinder further communication. Generally, the most common and polite way to address a person is to use "surname + title". Note that "title" here usually refers to official title, position, profession or academic title, instead of honorifics such as "Mr, Miss or Ms".

Do note that the Chinese will not address someone by his/her "surname" alone. It is also rare for the Chinese to address someone by his/her full name when they first meet, especially on formal social occasions, as it seems unfriendly and impolite. It is also inappropriate to address someone you just met by his/her given name, unless you are older or your status is higher, and you are trying to establish a closer relationship with him/her.

名不正则言不顺。称谓体现了人们之间的远近、亲疏、位次和隶属等关系，正确、得体的称谓在中国人的交往中起着非常重要的作用，不恰当的称呼可能会直接影响到双方进一步的交往。一般情况下，最常用、礼貌的称呼方法是“姓＋头衔”。注意这里的“头衔”一般是指官衔、职务、职业、学位等，而不是“先生、小姐、女士”。

请注意，中国人不单独用“姓”来称呼对方，初次见面时以全名来称呼也是少见的，尤其是正式

的社交场合，因为这显得既不友好，也没有礼貌。刚认识时也不适合用“名”来称呼，除非称呼者比被称呼者年长或职位高一些，而且想用这种方式来拉近彼此间的距离。

Lǐ lǎoshī
李老师

★★★ *Teacher Li*

Chén huìzhǎng
陈会长

★★★ *President Chen (of an association/society/council)*

Wáng júzhǎng
王局长

★★★ *Director-General Wang*

Liú jīnglǐ
刘经理

★★★ *Manager Liu*

Mǎ yīshēng
马医生

★★★ *Doctor Ma*

Wú bóshì
吴博士

★★★ *Dr. Wu (Ph.D. or doctorate)*

Wáng zǒng
王 总

★★★ *General Manager Wang*

Hú xiānsheng
胡 先 生

★★★ *Mr Hu*

Gāo xiǎojiě
高 小 姐

★★★ *Miss Gao*

Lín nǚshì
林 女 士

★★★★ *Ms Lin*

Lǐ
● 李

Li (surname)

Huá
● 华

Hua (given name)

Lǐ Huá
● 李 华

Li Hua (full name)

03 How to address someone you know well
怎么称呼熟悉的人

For friends whom you know well, you can usually address them by their given names only. However, people with one-syllable given names, regardless of their gender, should not be addressed by their given names, as it sounds too intimate. For people whom you are familiar with, you can address them by their full names, provided that they are similar in age and status as you. Otherwise it may still sound a bit offensive to them.

You can also address people by adding the prefixes "lǎo (old)" (mainly used on males) or "xiǎo (little)" before one's surname based on the difference in age between you and them. You can use "lǎo + surname" to address a middle-aged or elderly people of your age. You can use "xiǎo + surname" for someone who is obviously younger than you.

熟悉的朋友之间互相称呼，常常只叫名，不叫姓。但是要注意，对单名的人——无论是对同性还是异性，都不宜这么叫，因为这样称呼会显得过于亲昵。

对很熟悉的人，可以用全名来称呼，但是要与自己的年龄、职位差不多或者比自己年长、职位高一些，否则也会有冒犯的感觉。

还可以根据对方年龄和自己的年龄差距，把同龄的中老年人叫作“老＋姓”（主要用于男性），把明显比自己小的叫作“小＋姓”。

Bīnbīn
彬彬

★★ *Binbin*

Lǎo Liú
老刘

★★ *Old Liu*

Xiǎo Fàn
小范

★★ *Little Fan*

Lǐ Huá
李华

★ *Li Hua (full name)*

Dàwěi
大伟

★★ *Dawei*

04 How to address a stranger 怎么称呼陌生人

To break the ice between strangers, you can address them by a family-member title such as "dàmā (aunt)", "dàgē (elder brother)" or "dàjiě (elder sister)". The term "shīfu (sir)" is also a typical form of address for a male stranger in China, but it may seem a little outdated for young people. In addition, new

Internet words that are popular among young people, including "shuàigē(handsome man), měinǚ (beautiful woman), měiméi (pretty girl)" can be used on casual circumstances.

Tip: Use the term "xiǎojiě (miss)" with caution, as it has the negative meaning of "prostitute" when used alone.

中国人为了拉近相互间的距离，可以借用亲属称谓来称呼陌生人，如“大妈、大哥、大姐”；叫陌生人“师傅”也很有中国特色，不过对年轻人来说可能有点老套。在年轻人中很流行的网络新词“帅哥、美女、美眉”可以用在较为随意的场合。

请注意，小心使用“小姐”这个词，单独使用时带有“妓女”的负面意义。

dàye
大爷

★★ *uncle (generally older than your father)*

dàmā
大妈

★★ *aunt (similar age to your mother)*

dàshū
大叔

★★ *uncle (similar age to your father)*

āyí
阿姨

★★★ *aunt(similar age as your mother)*

dàgē
大哥

★★ *brother*

dàjiě
大姐

★★ *sister(must be obviously older than you)*

shīfu
师傅

★★ *sir/master(better be used on males)*

měinǚ
美女

★★ *beautiful woman*

shuàigē
帅哥

★★ *handsome man*

xiǎojiě
● 小姐

miss (when used alone as a form of address without following a surnane, it may mean prostitute)

05 How to exchange greetings with someone you first meet
初次见面怎么寒暄

When people first meet, they usually say hello to each other first, then they make some polite remarks or compliments such as “nice to meet you” or “I have heard a lot about you”. At times, people will also request humbly for the other party to take care of them.

初次见面，双方一般是相互问好，说些客气话，或者夸赞对方的话，比如“认识你很高兴”，或者“早就听说你了”之类的话；有的时候也谦虚地表达让对方关照自己的意思。

Nǐ hǎo !
你 好！

★★★ *Hello!*

Nín hǎo !
您 好！

★★★★ *Hello!*

Zǎoshang/ xiàwǔ /wǎnshang hǎo !
早 上 / 下 午 / 晚 上 好！

★★★ *Good morning/afternoon/evening!*

Rènshi nǐ hěn gāoxìng ! (Wǒ yě shì .)
认识你很 高兴！（我也是。）

★★★★ *Nice to meet you!(Me too.)*

Rènshi nín hěn róngxìng !
认识您 很 荣 幸！

★★★★★ *It is my honour to meet you!*

Zǎojiù tīngshuōguò nín le !
早就 听说过 您了！

★★★★ *I have heard a lot about you!*

Chū cì jiànmiàn , qǐng duō guānzhào !
初次见面，请 多 关照！

★★★★★ *We're meeting for the first time and I'd appreciate your help/guidance!*

Jiǔ wén dà míng !
久闻大 名！

★★★★★ *Your name has been known to me for a long time!*

06 How to exchange greetings with someone you know well
熟悉的人怎么寒暄

People who know each other well often ask simple questions which seem rather personal, such as "have you eaten" or "where are you going". However, the person who asks the question does not actually care about the answer, so the reply can be very casual. People who are familiar with each other may also ask yes-no questions about what they are doing, such as "are you reading?"

If you have not seen each other for a long time, you should usually ask how they have been lately. Many Chinese learners' pet phrase "Nǐ hǎo ma (How are you)" is actually not used among people who are familiar with each other. This greeting is only used between people who haven't been in touch for a long time, such as a pair of lovers who have broken up, and a time noun is often used here to help complete this sentence. So if you address a person with whom you are familiar using "Nǐ hǎo ma," he/she may feel awkward, although he/she will not say this outright.

比较熟悉的人之间可以问些看似私密的简单问

题，比如“吃饭了吗”“去哪里”，但实际上问话人并不真的关心答案，回答可以很随意；熟人之间还可以对对方正在做的事进行是非问，比如“在看书啊”，只需要肯定或者否定回答就可以了。

如果有段时间没有见面的熟人，再见时双方一定会相互问候一下近况。这里有一个误区，很多中文学习者常爱用“你好吗？”其实这个口头禅并不用于熟人之间，一般只用在很久没有联络的人之间（比如分手的恋人），而且常常加上时间名词，所以用这句话来问候熟悉的人会让对方觉得很别扭，虽然他们不会说出来。

Chī le ma ?
吃了吗？

★★ *Have you eaten?*

Qù nǎr a ?
去哪儿啊？

★★ *Where are you going?*

Sànbù ne ?
散步呢？

★★ *Taking a stroll?*

Jìnlái / Zuìjìn zěnme yàng ?
近来/最近怎么样？

★★★ *How have you been recently?*

Zhè duàn shíjiān hái hǎo ba ?
这段时间还好吧？

★★★ *How is everything going with you these days?*

Hǎo jiǔ bú jiàn le .
好久不见了。

★★★ *Long time no see!*

Yǒu duàn shíjiān méi jiàndào nǐ le !
有段时间没见到你了！

★★★ *It has been quite a long time since we've seen each other!*

Nǐ hǎo ma ?
● 你好吗？

How are you?

07 How to extend invitations
怎么发出邀请

Invitations can include both casual verbal ones, such as asking people out for a meal or movie, and formal written ones, such as inviting people to attend meetings or participate in activities. The tone used in written invitations is usually very polite, and some elegant wording and terms of respect are usually used.

邀请，既有比较随意的口头邀请，如一起吃饭、看电影，也有比较正式的书面邀请，如出席会议、参加活动。这时，邀请的语气一般都非常客气，会用到一些雅词和敬辞。

Wǎnshang yǒu kòng ma ?
晚上有空吗？

★★ *Are you free tonight?*

Wǎnshang nǐn yǒu ānpái ma ?
晚上您有安排吗？

★★★★ *Do you have anything on tonight?*

Wǎnshang yìqǐ qù kàn diànyǐng zěnme yàng ?
晚上一起去看电影怎么样？

★★ *What about watching a movie together tonight?*

Kěyǐ shǎngguāng chī dùn fàn ma ?
可以赏光吃顿饭吗？

★★★★ *May I have the honour of taking you out for lunch/dinner?*

Xīwàng nín néng guānglín jīntiān de wǎnhuì .
希望您能光临今天的晚会。

★★★★★ *We would appreciate your presence at the party tonight!*

Xīwàng nín néng zài bǎi máng zhī zhōng guānglín zhǐdǎo .
希望您能在百忙之中光临指导。

★★★★★ *We would appreciate it if you could take the time to be present and offer any advice.*

Hěn róngxìng de yāoqǐng nín cānjiā ...
很荣幸地邀请您参加……

★★★★★ *It is our honour to invite you to attend....*

08 How to welcome guests at home
怎么迎接家里的客人

Chinese people are very hospitable. They generally wait at the door to welcome the guests, ask about their trip, lead them into the house, invite them to take a seat and serve tea.

中国人很好客。客人即将到来时，主人一般会

站在门口迎接，并问候客人旅途的情况，请客人进屋，并让座、倒茶。

Xīkè xīkè !
稀客稀客！

★★ *(Such a) rare visitor!*

Nǐ kě shì xīkè a !
你可是稀客啊！

★★ *You are really a rare visitor!*

Kuài qǐng jìn !
快 请 进！

★★ *Please come in!*

Kuài jìn wū ba !
快进屋吧！

★★ *Please come into the house!*

Yí lù xīnkǔ le !
一路辛苦了！

★★★ *You must have had a tiring trip!*

Lù shang xīnkǔ le !
路 上 辛苦了！

★★★ *You must have had a tiring trip!*

Lù shang hái shùnlì ba ?
路 上 还顺利吧？

★★★ *Did you have a good trip?*

09 How to introduce your family members

怎么介绍家人

When introducing one's family members, one should choose the appropriate forms of address based on the relationship between the two parties. They should not be too causal on formal occasions; neither should they be too formal on everyday occasions. For example,

"fùqin/mǔqin (father/mother)" are elegant words used in written language. They should only be used verbally on solemn occasions; otherwise, it may seem rather weird.

介绍自己家人的时候，要根据双方之间的关系来选用不同的家庭成员称谓，原则是正式场合不能太随意，平常场合也不能太正式。比如"父亲 / 母亲"属于书面语的雅词，只有在庄重的场合才会用在口头上，否则就会显得比较奇怪。

Zhè shì wǒ bà / mā .
这是我爸 / 妈。

★★ *This is my dad/mum.*

Zhè shì wǒ lǎobà / lǎomā .
这是我老爸 / 老妈。

★★ *This is my daddy/mummy.*

Zhè shì wǒ bàba / māma .
这是我爸爸 / 妈妈。

★★★ *This is my dad/mum.*

Zhè wèi shì wǒ fùqin / mǔqin .
这位是我父亲 / 母亲。

★★★★ *This is my father/mother.*

Zhè shì wǒ lǎogōng / lǎopo .
这是我老公 / 老婆。

★★ *This is my husband/wife.*

Zhè shì wǒ zhàngfu / qīzi .
这是我丈夫/妻子。

★★★ *This is my husband/wife.*

Zhè shì wǒ àiren .
这是我爱人。

★★★ *This is my husband/wife.*

Zhè wèi shì wǒ xiānsheng .
这位是我先生。

★★★★ *This is my husband.*

Zhè shì wǒ tàitai .
这是我太太。

★★★★ *This is my wife.*

Zhè wèi shì wǒ fūren .
这位是我夫人。

★★★★★ *This is my wife.*

Zhè shì wǒ jiā de lǎo dà / lǎo èr .
这是我家的老大/老二。

★★ *This is my oldest/second child.*

Zhè shì wǒ de dà nǚ'ér .
这是我的大女儿。

★★★ *This is my elder/eldest daughter.*

10 How to give and receive gifts 怎么送收礼物

Choosing the appropriate gift is very important, but knowing what to say in giving a gift is equally important. To avoid making a recipient uneasy, Chinese people will usually modestly say that the gifts are inexpensive.

When receiving gifts, Chinese people will often attempt to refuse them out of politeness. Even if they accept a gift, they will not open the gift in front of the gift-giver. Moreover, gift-givers are also often

unaccustomed to being present when the gift they have given is opened. However, young people nowadays are getting used to Western etiquette. They often open gifts in front of the gift-givers and pay compliments to them.

选择合适的礼物很重要，但是送的时候怎么说也很重要。中国人这时一般会自谦地说礼物不贵重，以免引起对方的不安。如果要去中国人家里，带一些小礼物是适宜的。

中国人收到礼物时常常会客气地推辞一下。收下礼物后也不习惯当面打开，有时候送礼的人也不希望对方当面打开。不过，现在年轻人已经习惯了西方的方式，也常常当面打开礼物并且加以赞美。

Yìdiǎnr xiǎo yìsi, qǐng nín shōuxià.
一点儿小意思，请您收下。

★★★★ *A small token of appreciation, please accept it.*

Yìdiǎnr xīnyì.
一点儿心意。

★★★ *A small token of appreciation.*

Yě bù zhīdào nín xǐhuan shénme.
也不知道您喜欢什么。

★★★★ *I'm not sure what you would prefer.*

Bù chéng jìngyì, qǐng nín xiàonà.
不成敬意，请您笑纳。

★★★★★ *A little token to show my respect, please accept it.*

Kèqi shénme ya!
客气什么呀！

★★★ *Why so courteous?*

Sòng nǐ ge lǐwù, xīwàng nǐ xǐhuan.
送你个礼物，希望你喜欢。

★★★ *I have a gift for you, and I hope you like it.*

Xīnyì lǐngle jiù xíng le.
心意领了就行了。

★★★ *I am grateful for your thoughtfulness!*

Hái dài shénme lǐwù a!
还带什么礼物啊！

★★★ *You didn't have to bring a gift!*

Nǐ tài kèqi le!
你太客气了！

★★★ *You are too kind!*

Xièxie zhēn piàoliang!
谢谢！真漂亮！

★★★ *Thank you! It is very beautiful!*

11 How to compliment others
怎么夸奖对方

Chinese people are modest and restrained when complimenting their family members, but they are more direct and generous when praising other people. Nevertheless, you should still base what you say on facts and speak within proper limits to avoid being misunderstood as mocking someone or being sarcastic. Also, if you are complimenting someone's spouse who is of the opposite sex, it is best not to praise his/her look or dress to avoid making him/her uncomfortable.

和夸奖自己家人的自谦、内敛相比，中国人夸奖对方是很直接、慷慨的，但是也要注意客观事实和尺度，以免有讽刺挖苦的嫌疑。另外还要注意，你在夸奖对方的配偶，尤其还是异性时，最好不要过度夸奖其外貌和穿着，以免给对方不舒服的感觉。

Nǐ zhēn shuài / piàoliang !
你真帅 / 漂亮！

★★★ *You are very handsome/beautiful!*

Nǐ chuān de zhēn yǒu pǐnwèi .
你穿得真有品味。

★★★ *You have a good sense of style.*

Nǐ zhēn huì chuān yīfu .
你真会穿衣服。

★★★ *You certainly have an eye for clothes!*

Nǐ de yīfu shì zài nǎr mǎi de ?
你的衣服是在哪儿买的？

★★★ *Where did you buy your clothes?*

Nǐ de qìzhì zhēn hǎo !
你的气质真好！

★★★ *You have a great disposition!*

Nǐ de Zhōngwén shuō de tài bàng le !
你的中文说得太棒了！

★★★ *You speak Chinese very fluently!*

12 How to respond to praise
怎么应对夸奖

Abiding by the principle of modesty, Chinese people tend to humbly deny praises that are directed towards them. Sometimes they may even respond by making self-deprecating remarks or elevating the statuses of other people. The same applies when compliments are given to their family members or

possessions.

But today more and more people are getting used to responding with “thank you”.

中国人听到夸奖自己、自己的家人，以及自己的物品时，一般会遵循自谦的原则，谦虚地表示其实不够好，有时甚至会有意地自我贬损，以抬高对方。

不过现在人们受西方文化影响，越来越习惯回答“谢谢”。

Yìbān ba .
一般吧。

★★★ *Not bad.*

Bù gǎn dāng .
不敢当。

★★★★ *I really don't deserve this.*

Wǒ hái chà de yuǎn .
我还差得远。

★★★ *There is still a long way to go for me.*

Nǎli nǎli .
哪里哪里。

★★★ *I'm flattered.*

Mǎmahūhū ba .
马马虎虎吧。

★★★ *Just so-so.*

Bù néng hé nǐ xiāngbǐ .
不能和你相比。

★★★★ *(This is) nothing compared to you.*

Wǒ yàoshi yǒu nǐ zhème hǎo de gōngzuò jiù hǎo le !
我要是有你这么好的工作就好了！

★★★★ *If only I had a job as good as yours!*

Nǐ de Zhōngwén cái shuō de hǎo !
你的中文才说得好！

★★★★ *Your Chinese is really fluent!*

Chéngméng kuājiǎng .
承蒙夸奖。

★★★★ *I'm flattered by your compliments.*

Nín guòjiǎng le !
您过奖了！

★★★★ *You flatter me.*

Xièxie !
谢谢！

★★★ *Thank you!*

Xièxie nín de kěndìng .
谢谢您的肯定。

★★★ *Thanks for your recognition.*

13 How to praise those close to you
怎么夸奖自己人

Abiding by the principle of modesty, Chinese people tend to use neutral words to weaken the intention of a compliment, as well as a casual tone such as "Not too bad" when praising people closely related to them. They will not praise their children in front of people whom they are not familiar with, neither will they praise their spouses directly. Instead, sometimes they may

convey the shortcomings of their own people by praising others.

遵循自谦的原则，中国人在夸奖自家人时常常使用中性词，来淡化夸奖的意思；语气上也常常显得随意，如“还行吧”。在不太熟悉的人面前，中国人更不会夸奖自己的孩子、妻子或者丈夫，有时候还可能会通过夸奖对方的方式来指出自家人的不足之处。

Wǒ nánpéngyou de gōngzuò hái xíng / kěyǐ ba .
我男朋友的工作还行 / 可以吧。

★★★ *My boyfriend's job is Okay/ all right.*

Tā de Yīngyǔ yìbānbān / mǎmahūhū ba .
他的英语一般般 / 马马虎虎吧。

★★★ *His English is just Okay/so-so.*

Tā de gōngzuò bǐ nǐ chàyuǎn le .
他的工作比你差远了。

★★★ *Your job is far better than his!*

Wǒ qīzi zhǎng de hěn piàoliang .
● 我妻子长得很漂亮。

My wife is very beautiful.

Wǒ zhè jiàn yīfu hěn piàoliang ba ?
● 我这件衣服很漂亮吧？

Aren't my clothes beautiful?

14 How to ask someone's age
怎么问年龄

It is safe to ask Chinese about their age, although well-educated female adults living in the cities may be reluctant to give an answer. On the other hand, it may be a good question to ask the elders, because asking about their age shows that you are concerned about their health. However, the way you ask should be determined by the difference in age or status between you and the other party. Never ask an elderly person in the same manner as you would ask a child because it is very disrespectful.

Common ways of asking include, 1) for people younger than you, especially children, you may ask "nǐ jīn nián jǐ suì"; 2) for people who are about the same age as you, you may ask "nǐ jīn nián duō dà"; 3) for people who are obviously older than you, you may ask "nín jīn nián duō dà suìshù/niánjì". Another clever and uniquely Chinese way of asking is to ask for their zodiac animal. However, you will need to know the cycle of the 12 animals in order to work out the age.

问中国人年龄并不是件冒险的事，虽然教育程度高的现代女性可能不愿意回答，但对年长者来说，很可能是个好问题，因为这意味着你关心其健康状况。但是，问年龄要根据双方之间的年龄差距和地位关系把握询问方式和语气，千万不能用问小孩子的方式来问年长者，那样会非常不尊敬。

常用的问法有：一、对比自己年龄小的人，尤其是小孩子，可以问“你今年几岁”；二、对和自己相差不大的人可以问“你今年多大”；三、对比自己

明显年长的人，可以问“您今年多大岁数 / 年纪”。当然，还有一种很聪明而且很有中国特色的问法，即问对方的属相，不过你得知道怎么换算。

Nǐ jīnnián jǐ suì ?
你今年几岁？

★★★ *How old are you?(mainly for children)*

Nǐ jīnnián duō dà ?
你今年多大？

★★★ *How old are you?(for people of your age)*

Nǐ shǔ shénme ?
你属什么？

★★★ *What is your zodiac animal?*

Nǐ shì nǎ yì nián de ?
你是哪一年的？

★★★ *Which year were you born in?*

Nín jīnnián duō dà suìshù / niánjì ?
您今年多大岁数 / 年纪？

★★★★ *How old are you? (for the elderly)*

Nín jīnnián gāoshòu ?
您今年高寿？

★★★★★ *How old are you?(for the elderly)*

Kěyǐ zhīdào nín jīnnián duō dà ma ?
可以知道您今年多大吗？

★★★★ *May I know how old you are?*

15 How to welcome customers
怎么接待餐馆的顾客

When waiters or waitresses at restaurants receive customers, they often ask for the number of guests, table reservations, and so on, so as to arrange seating or private rooms accordingly. Private dining rooms are very common in Chinese restaurants. The main benefit of such rooms is that the hosts and guests can interact and dine in private without being disturbed.

餐馆服务员迎接顾客时，常常会问有几位、是否预订了座位之类的问题，她们会根据人数和客人需要来安排座位或包间。包间在中国较为常见，其好处是主客可以安静交流而不被打扰。

Huānyíng guānglín !
欢迎光临！

★★★★ *Welcome!*

Qǐng jìn / zuò !
请进/坐！

★★★★ *Please come in /take a seat!*

Qǐngwèn nín yǒu jǐ wèi ?
请问您有几位？

★★★★ *May I know how many people there are?*

Qǐngwèn nín yùdìng zuòwei le ma ?
请问您预订座位了吗？

★★★★ *Have you made a table reservation?*

Qǐngwèn nín xiǎng chī / hē diǎnr shénme ?
请问您想吃/喝点儿什么？

★★★★ *What would you like to eat/drink?*

Xiànzài shì liǎnghūn-sānsù .
现在是两荤三素。

★★★ *(There are) two meat and three vegetable dishes currently.*

Zhè shì wǒmen de zhāo paí cài .
这是我们的招牌菜。

★★★ *This is our signature dish.*

Hái yào bié de ma ?
还 要别的吗？

★★★ *Would you like anything else?*

Hái yào diǎnr shénme ma ?
还 要点儿什么 吗？

★★★ *Would you like to order anything else?*

Bú gòu dehuà zài diǎn ba .
不 够 的话 再 点 吧。

★★★ *Order more if it is not enough.*

Nǐmen chī shénme ?
● 你们吃什么？

What do you want to eat?

16 How to order food
怎么点菜

As a sign of respect, hosts usually invite guests to order food first. When they do so, it is advisable to decline a little. After ordering one or two dishes, it is best to give someone else the chance to do so, too. When ordering dishes, you should consider everyone's tastes and preferences, as Chinese food is usually shared among everyone at the table.

主人为表示尊敬，一般会请客人先点菜，这时候客人略微推辞一下比较好；客人点了一两个菜后

也可以让其他人点菜。点菜的时候也要适当考虑大家的口味，因为中餐是分享式的。

Nǐ xiān diǎn .
你先点。

★★★ *You order first.*

Háishi nǐ xiān / lái diǎn ba .
还是你先/来点吧。

★★★ *(No,) you order first.*

Wǒ bù shúxi zhèli de kǒuwèi .
我不熟悉这里的口味。

★★★ *I am not familiar with the taste of the food here.*

Nǐ néng chī là de ma ?
你能吃辣的吗？

★★★ *Can you eat spicy food?*

Néng chī yìdiǎnr / bù néng chī là de .
能吃一点儿/不能吃辣的。

★★★ *I can eat a little/I can't eat spicy food.*

Nǐ yǒu jì kǒu ma
你有忌口吗？

★★★ *Do you avoid certain food?*

Wǒ dōu kěyǐ chī . / Wǒ bù chī zhūròu .
我都可以吃。/我不吃猪肉。

★★★ *I'm OK with any food. /I don't eat pork.*

Yào / Lái yí ge suānlàyú .
要/来一个酸辣鱼。

★★★ *(I'd) want/like one spicy and sour fish.*

Zài lái yí ge fānqiéchǎodàn .
再来一个番茄炒蛋。

★★★ *And a scrambled egg with tomatoes.*

Yǒu jǐ ge cài le ?
有几个菜了？

★★★ *How many dishes are there?*

Nǐmen yǒu shénme tèsècài ma ?
你们 有 什么特色菜吗？

★★★ *What are your specialty dishes?*

Lái diǎnr shénme zhǔshí ?
来点儿什么 主食？

★★★ *What staple food shall we order?*

Xūyào dehuà zàidiǎn .
需要的话 再点。

★★★ *Order more if needed.*

17 How to entertain guests
怎么招待客人

The modesty of Chinese people is also reflected at the dining table. Even if there are many delicacies available, Chinese hosts will say humbly that there is not enough food or the food is not good enough. They will eagerly urge their guests to take more, and sometimes they may even zealously give food to them.

When a host gives food to you, it is appropriate to first politely decline a little, but eventually accept it. Of course, you can also refuse politely. Praising the host's

culinary skills or complimenting the food will make him/her very happy.

中国人的自谦也体现在餐桌上。即便桌子上有很多好吃的菜，中国主人仍会谦虚地说没有什么菜，或者菜做得不好。他们会殷勤地劝客人多吃菜，有的时候还会热情地给客人夹菜。

主人给客人夹菜的时候，客人礼貌地推辞一下，恭敬接受是很得体的，当然也可以有礼貌地谢绝。客人适时对主人的厨艺或者菜品夸奖一番，会让主人很高兴。

Nà wǒmen kāishǐ ba !
那我们开始吧！

★★★ *Let's eat!*

Lái chángchang zhè ge cài .
来尝尝这个菜。

★★★ *Try this dish.*

Dōu shì xiē jiāchángcài .
都是些家常菜。

★★★★ *(These are) merely home-style dishes.*

Méi shénme cài, suíbiàn chī diǎnr ba.
没什么菜，随便吃点儿吧。

★★★★ *There're not many dishes, but help yourself.*

Zhè ge cài gòu de zháo ma?
这个菜够得着吗？

★★★ *Can you reach this dish?*

Duō chī diǎnr.
多吃点儿。

★★★ *Eat more.*

Suíbiàn chī, bié kèqi.
随便吃，别客气。

★★★ *Help yourself to the food, you don't have to be polite.*

Zài chī diǎnr ba.
再吃点儿吧。

★★★ *Eat a little more.*

Wǒ bú kèqi le, zìjǐ lái.
我不客气了，自己来。

★★★ *You can relax, I'll help myself (to the food).*

Tài hǎochī le!
太好吃了！

★★★ *It's very delicious!*

18 How to drink the proper way
怎么喝酒

A banquet without alcohol is no banquet at all, as the Chinese saying goes. When Chinese people host dinners, they generally will urge their guests to drink some spirits. However, under the influence of Western culture, a host will not insist if the guests make it known that they cannot drink. Even if you can drink some spirits, it is still advisable for you to decline a little. It is best to wait till the host raises his/her glass and invites everyone to drink before you start drinking it. When dinner is ongoing, try not to drink on your own. It is polite to invite someone seated next to you to drink together.

When the host pours you another glass of spirits, you may extend your hand (with your palm facing the glass) to express thanks.When pouring spirits for others, always fill the cup to the brim as a sign of respect.

When Chinese make a toast, they will usually hold the cup with two hands, therefore it is best if you follow suit. Otherwise it will make you appear arrogant. As an old tradition, you can use one hand to gently lift another person's cup to a level higher than your own cup to show respect for the latter.

“无酒不成席”，中国人请客吃饭，一般都会劝客人喝点儿酒。不过受西方影响，客人如果表示自己不会喝，主人也不会勉强；如果喝的话，也适当推辞一下比较好。开始喝酒的时候，要等主人举起杯子邀请以后再喝比较好，席间最好不要自己一个人喝，邀请一下邻座会显得礼貌。主人来给客人斟酒时，你可以礼貌地伸出一只手（让手掌心靠近桌子上的酒杯）来表示感谢。

注意，主人倒酒的时候（白酒）要倒满，否则是不尊敬对方。

中国人敬酒的时候，为显示尊敬，一般都会站起来，用双手捧起酒杯。这时候你最好也用双手，

否则会显得高高在上。老的传统还会用一只手轻轻抬起对方的酒杯，使其高于自己的酒杯，以显示尊敬对方。

Nín hē diǎnr shénme ?
您喝点儿什么？

★★★★ *What would you like to drink?*

Lái bēi báijiǔ zěnme yàng ?
来杯白酒怎么样？

★★★ *How about a cup of Chinese alcohol?*

Lái yì bēi ba .
来一杯吧。

★★★ *One cup, please.*

Wǒ jìng nín yì bēi !
我敬您一杯！

★★★★★ *Allow me to offer a toast to you!*

Gānbēi !
干杯！

★★★ *Cheers!*

Zài lái yì bēi !
再来一杯！

★★★ *Have another cup!*

Wèile wǒmen de hézuò , gān yì bēi !
为了我们的合作，干一杯！

★★★ *Let's drink a toast to our partnership!*

19 How to leave the table early
怎么提前离席

If you finish eating first, you should generally notify the hosts and other guests such that they can continue eating and drinking at ease. If you have something to attend to and need to leave the table early, be sure to explain yourself well to avoid making anyone feel awkward when you leave. By doing so, people won't think that you are self-centered or that you do not care about other people.

Tip: It is not advisable for the hosts themselves to finish eating first.

你如果先吃完，一般要和还在吃的主人和其他客人打个招呼，让大家继续安心喝酒、吃饭；如果因为有事需要提前离开，一定要做好解释工作，以

免自己离开让大家觉得冷场，并且避免给人留下只管自己、不管别人的不好印象。

请注意，主人最好不要自己先吃完离席。

Gèwèi mànyòng, wǒ chī hǎo le.
各位慢用，我吃好了。

★★★★ *Please carry on eating, everyone, I've finished eating.*

Wǒ chī hǎo le, nín mànmàn chī.
我吃好了，您慢慢吃。

★★★★ *I've finished eating, please carry on.*

Nín màn yòng.
您慢用。

★★★★ *Please carry on.*

Wǒ chī bǎo le.
我吃饱了。

★★ *I'm full.*

Gèwèi mànmàn chī, wǒ yǒu diǎnr shì xiān zǒu le.
各位慢慢吃，我有点儿事先走了。

★★★★ *Please carry on eating, everyone, I have something to attend to and have to leave now.*

Bàoqiàn, shīpéi le.
抱歉，失陪了。

★★★★ *Sorry, excuse me for leaving early.*

Bù hǎoyìsi, wǒ xiān zǒu yí bù.
不好意思，我先走一步。

★★★ *I'm sorry, I'm going make a move.*

20 How to pay the bill
怎么买单

Chinese people are very hospitable. When friends dine out together, someone usually takes the initiative to foot the bill and may even rush to pay the bill first, if it is not agreed beforehand who picks up the tab. So if you would like to treat your guests to a meal, it is best to make it clear at the outset.

Tip: If someone excuses himself/herself while taking the meal, they may go to the washroom, but they may also go to pay the bill. So if you do not want him/her to foot the bill, it is best to look and see what he/she is doing.

中国人很好客，朋友们一起在外面吃饭的时候，如果没有说好谁买单，中国人常常会主动买单，甚至会抢着买单，所以如果你想请客的话，最好开始就说清楚。

提示：在吃饭中途，如果有人出去一会儿，他可能是去卫生间，也很有可能是去买单哦！所以如果你不想让他买单的话，最好去外面看一下。

Jīntiān wǒ qǐngkè .
今天我请客。

★★★ *Today is my treat today.*

Wǒ lái mǎidān .
我来买单。

★★★ *Let me foot the bill.*

Yàobu wǒmen AA-zhì ba .
要不我们AA制吧。

★★★ *Let's go Dutch.*

Zěnme néng ràng nǐ qǐngkè / mǎidān ne ?
怎么能让你请客/买单呢？

★★★ *How can I let you treat (me)/foot the bill?*

Shuōhǎo wǒ mǎidān de !
说好我买单的！

★★★ *It is agreed that I'm footing the bill!*

Nǐ shì kèren , bú yòng guǎn .
你是客人，不用管。

★★★ *You are my guest, do not worry (with the bill).*

Doū bié zhēng le wǒ shì dìzhǔ , gāi wǒ qǐng .
都别争了，我是地主，该我请。

★★★ *Stop arguing, I am the host, I will pay.*

Xià cì nǐ zài qǐng ba .
下次你再请吧。

★★★ *You pay next time.*

Wǒ yǐjīng mǎiguò le .
我已经买过了。

★★★ *I have paid.*

Nà gǎitiān wǒ lái qǐng !
那改天我来请！

★★ *Then I shall treat you another time.*

Nà wǒ jiù gōngjìng bùrú cóngmìng le .
那我就恭敬不如从命了。

★★★★ *In that case, I shall not stand on ceremony.*

21 How to bid farewell to the host
怎么和主人告别

If you are a guest, it is improper to leave too early. You generally have a chat with the host before saying goodbye. Usually you leave with a good reason or sometimes a good excuse.

Chinese hosts usually ask their guests to stay longer one or two times, and the latter may decide according to the situation whether to stay longer. If the hosts truly hope you stay longer and you can do so, then you should give them "face" and stay on.

如果你是去做客，不宜过早告别。一般吃完饭后你要和主人聊聊天再提出告别。提早告别通常会说个理由，

有时候只是找个借口。

中国主人一般都会挽留客人一两次，客人可以根据情况，决定是否再逗留一会儿。如果主人确实希望你多留一会儿，而你自己也可以，那就给个“面子”吧。

Shí jiān bùzǎo le, wǒ děi zǒu le.
时间不早了，我得走了。

★★★ *It is getting late, I have to leave.*

Míngtiān hái yào shàngbān, wǒ děi zǒu le.
明天还要上班，我得走了。

★★★ *I have to work tomorrow, I have to leave.*

Míngtiān nǐ hái yǒu shì, jiù bù dǎrǎo le!
明天你还有事，就不打扰了！

★★★ *You are busy tomorrow, I shall not disturb you further!*

Bùzǎo le, zhēn de děi zǒu le.
不早了，真的得走了。

★★★ *It is getting late, I really have to leave.*

Dǎrǎo bàntiān le, nǐ yě zǎo diǎnr xiūxi.
打扰半天了，你也早点儿休息。

★★★ *I have called upon you for half a day, I shall leave now so that you can get some rest.*

Cái qī diǎn , zài wán yíhuìr ba .
才七点，再玩一会儿吧。

★★★ *It is just 7 pm, (let's) hang out a little longer.*

Míngtiān zhōumò , zháo shénme jí a ?
明天周末，着什么急啊？

★★★ *It is the weekend tomorrow, what's the hurry?*

Hǎo jiǔ bú jiàn le , zài wán yíhuìr ba .
好久不见了，再玩一会儿吧。

★★★ *It's been a long time since we met, (let's) hang out a little longer.*

Zháo shénme jí a , hái zǎo ne !
着什么急啊，还早呢！

★★★ *What's the hurry, it's still early!*

Nándé jiànshang yí miàn , zài liáo huìr ba .
难得见上一面，再聊会儿吧。

★★★ *We don't often see each other, let us chat more.*

Xià cì hái bù zhīdào shénme shíhou néng jiàndào ne !
下次还不知道什么时候能见到呢！

★★★ *Who knows when we can meet again?*

22 How to see guests off
怎么送客人

Chinese people usually see their guests to the door, and even continue to accompany them for a few steps beyond the door. Not only will hosts urge their guests to take good care of themselves, the former will also extend good wishes to the latter and express the hope of another visit. Usually hosts will return to their homes only after seeing their guests drive off.

If guests are waiting for transport or for flights, the

hosts may also accompany them. In such cases, guests should find an opportune moment to let their hosts know they do not need to wait longer, so as not to take up too much of their hosts' time.

中国人一般会送客人出门，并陪着走几步，同时好意地嘱咐、祝福，希望客人再来做客，直到看着客人开车或坐车离开后才回去。

客人如果等车或飞机的话，主人也可能会陪着等，客人可以适时请主人不要再送或再等，以免耽误主人过多时间。

Màn zǒu .
慢 走。

★★★ *Take care.*

Nín màn zǒu .
您 慢 走。

★★★★ *Mind how you go.*

Yǒu kòng zài lái wánr .
有 空 再 来 玩 儿。

★★★ *Come again when you are free.*

Zhāodài bù zhōu , qǐng duō bāohán .
招 待 不 周 ， 请 多 包 涵。

★★★★★ *Please forgive me, my hospitality is not good enough.*

Zhù nǐ yí lù píng'ān .
祝你一路平安。

★★★★ *Wish you a safe trip.*

Zhù nǐ yí lù shùnfēng .
祝你一路顺风。

★★★★ *Wish you a smooth trip. (Note: This is not said to someone taking a flight as tailwinds can be a hazard.)*

Nà wǒ bú sòng le .
那我不送了。

★★★ *I shall not send you off then.*

Lù shang zhùyì ānquán .
路上注意安全。

★★★ *Pay attention to safety on the roads!*

Bǎochí liánxì .
保持联系。

★★★ *Keep in touch!*

Bié sòng le , huíqu ba .
别送了，回去吧。

★★★ *Don't send me off further, go home.*

Hǎo le , kuài huíqu ba .
好了，快回去吧。

★★★ *OK, hurry home please.*

Hǎo le , qǐng liúbù ba !
好了，请留步吧！

★★★ *OK, please stay where you are.*

23 How to congratulate children on their birthdays
怎么祝贺孩子的生日

Chinese people attach great importance to children's birthdays. Although important birthdays may vary from place to place, generally grand celebrations are held when babies are one month old and one year old. In some parts of China, people also have bigger birthday celebrations for three-year-olds and twelve-year-olds. On a first-year celebration, Chinese like to give a baby a grabbing test. Various items are spread before the baby. The item it grabs is said to foretell its future career.

Traditionally, on the morning of his/her birthday, a Chinese eats a bowl of longevity noodles which shows good blessings for him/her. However, a child may prefer

McDonald's to longevity noodles!

中国人对孩子的生日很重视，虽然各地重点过哪几个生日不太一样，但是一般都会非常隆重地庆祝满月和一周岁，有的地方还会庆祝三岁或者十二岁。小孩子满周岁时，中国人喜欢玩一个叫“抓周”的游戏，来预测孩子长大以后会从事什么行业。

中国人习惯在生日那天的早上吃一碗长寿面，象征着大家对“寿星”的美好祝福。不过今天的小孩子也许会更喜欢麦当劳吧！

Shēngrì kuàilè !
生日快乐！

★★★ *Happy Birthday!*

Zhù bǎobao jiànkāng chéngzhǎng !
祝宝宝健康成长！

★★★ *May the baby grow strong and healthy!*

Zhù bǎobèi tiāntiān kuàilè !
祝宝贝天天快乐！

★★★ *May the baby always be full of joy!*

Zhù nǐ xuéxí jìnbù !
祝你学习进步！

★★★ *May you make progress in your study!*

Zhù xiǎopéngyou tiāntiān xiàng shàng !
祝小朋友天天向上！

★★★ *May our young friend (s) make progress every day!*

24 How to congratulate adults on their birthdays
怎么祝贺成人的生日

To Chinese people, the zodiac year (běnmìngnián), which is any year of one's Chinese zodiac animal sign, bears much significance. The zodiac year falls every 12 years after one's birth, such as the years when one reaches 24, 36, 48, and 60. It is said that people tend to be vulnerable in their zodiac year, so they will

usually wear auspicious objects in red, such as wrist or ankle rope bracelets, in order to ward off any dangers. In addition, it is a taboo in many parts of China for men to celebrate their 30th birthdays and for women to celebrate their 40th birthdays. Because they are just at a critical juncture in their lives, they must be cautious.

Another thing meriting our attention is that birthdays are generally celebrated before or on the actual dates of birth. It is a no-no to have belated birthday celebrations.

对中国人来说，本命年具有特别重要的意义。本命年是指12的倍数年，如24岁、36岁、48岁、60岁。据说人在本命年比较脆弱，所以一般会穿戴红色的吉祥物（如手绳、脚绳）以求平安。此外，中国的很多地方都忌讳男人过30岁、女人过40岁的生日，因为这时他们正处于人生的关口，需要小心。

另外要注意，生日一般只能提前过，而不能推后过。

Zhù nǐ shēngrì kuàilè !
祝你生日快乐！

★★★ *Happy Birthday!*

Zhù nǐ yuè lái yuè shuài / piàoliang !
祝你越来越 帅 / 漂 亮 ！

★★★ *May you become more handsome/beautiful!*

Zhù nǐ yìfān-fēngshùn !
祝你一帆风顺！

★★★ *May everything go smoothly for you!*

Zhù nǐ wànshì-rúyì !
祝你万事如意！

★★★ *May all go well with you!*

Zhù nǐ xīnxiǎng-shìchéng !
祝你心想事成！

★★★ *May all your wishes come true!*

Zhù nǐ mèngxiǎng-chéngzhēn !
祝你梦想成真！

★★★ *May all your dreams come true!*

Zhù nǐ yuè huó yuè niánqīng !
祝你越活越年轻！

★★ *May you stay young forever!*

Gōngxǐ nǐ yòu zhǎng yí suì !
恭喜你又长一岁！

★★ *Congratulations on being one year older!*

25 How to congratulate elderly people on their birthdays 怎么祝贺老年人的生日

In China, middle-aged and elderly people generally prefer to celebrate their birthdays according to the lunar calendar rather than the Gregorian calendar, whereas young people are used to celebrating their birthdays according to the Gregorian calendar.

Respecting the elderly and loving the young is a long-standing Chinese tradition, therefore the birthday of an elderly person is an important occasion for the entire family. Generally, the first grand birthday begins at the age of 60. From then on, small (and rather grand) celebrations occur every five years while big (and very

grand) celebrations occur every ten years. On birthdays, the children of the elderly will invite friends and relatives to the ceremony, and the elderly will receive various birthday gifts.

It is interesting to note that in many parts of China, birthdays at multiples of ten are celebrated one year in advance (for example, a 60th birthday is celebrated when the person reaches 59 years old).

在中国，中老年人一般都喜欢过阴历而不是阳历的生日；年轻人则习惯过阳历的生日。

尊老爱幼是中国人的优良传统，所以老年人过生日对全家来说是件很重要的事情。第一个隆重的生日一般从60岁开始，以后5年一小庆（相当隆重），10年一大庆（非常隆重）。生日当天，子女们会邀请亲朋好友一起庆祝，老人会收到他们带来的各种礼物。

有意思的是，中国不少地方有这样一个传统，逢十的生日会提前一年过，比如60岁的生日是在59岁过。

Zhù nín shēngrì kuàilè !
祝您生日快乐！

★★★ *Wishing you a happy birthday!*

Zhù nín lǎo jiànkāng-chángshòu !
祝您老健康长寿！

★★★ *May you live to a ripe old age!*

Zhù lǎoshòuxing chángmìng-bǎisuì !
祝老寿星长命百岁！

★★★ *May lao shou xing (the elderly person whose birthday is being celebrated) enjoy good health and longevity!*

Zhù nín xiàokǒu-chángkāi !
祝您笑口常开！

★★★ *May you always wear a smile!*

Zhù nín shòubínánshān !
祝您寿比南山！

★★★★ *May you have a long life!*

Zhù nín fúrúdōnghǎi !
祝您福如东海！

★★★★ *May you have boundless happiness!*

26 How to extend New Year greetings 怎么祝贺春节

The Spring Festival is the most important festival in China. When people meet in the first month of the lunar New Year, they always exchange best wishes. On some special occasions such as a banquet, Chinese people extend wishes by bringing their two hands together in front of their chest, with the left palm over the right clenched fist, and saying at the same time auspicious words such as wishing one another prosperity, good luck and happiness. Inauspicious words, especially those related to disease and death, must not be spoken during the festival.

The Chinese people have a tradition of distributing red envelopes containing money as gifts to their younger generations during the New Year. This always delights both the recipient and the giver.

春节是中国最重要的节日。春节后的一个月内，人们见面都要相互祝福。在一些特定的场合如宴会上，中国人会用传统的方式来祝福，即双手举在胸前，右手握成拳头，左手包住右拳，同时说“恭喜发财、吉祥如意”之类的祝福话，避免说些不吉祥的话，尤其是病、死等词语。

过年的时候中国长辈有给晚辈发红包的传统，收红包的人开心，发的人也开心。

Guònián hǎo!
过年好！

★★★ *Happy New Year!*

Gěi nín bàinián la!
给您拜年啦！

★★★ *Wish you a happy New Year!*

Gōngxǐ fācái!
恭喜发财！

★★★ *May you have a prosperous New Year!*

Zhù nǐ gǒunián dàjí!
祝你狗年大吉！

★★★ *May you be very lucky in the Year of the Dog!*

Zhù nǐ xīnnián hǎoyùn!
祝你新年好运！

★★★ *Wishing you good luck in the New Year!*

Zhù nǐ cáiyuán-guǎngjìn!
祝你财源广进！

★★★ *May you have wide sources of revenue!*

Zhù nǐ shēngyi-xīnglóng!
祝你生意兴隆！

★★★ *May your business be brisk!*

Zhù nǐ wànshì-rúyì!
祝你万事如意！

★★★ *May all go well with you!*

Zhù nǐ xīnxiǎng-shìchéng!
祝你心想事成！

★★★ *May all your wishes come true!*

27 How to extend best wishes at important festivals
怎么祝福重要节日

The important traditional festivals in China include the Spring Festival, the Lantern Festival, the Qingming Day, the Dragon Boat Festival and the Mid-Autumn Festival. These five traditional festivals have different cultural elements and customs. At the Spring Festival and the Lantern Festival, people celebrate the New Year; at the Mid-Autumn Festival, the entire family reunites. So these three festivals are thought to be happy occasions and people can wish "Happy… Festival" to each other. At the Dragon Boat Festival, people pray for an ancient patriotic poet. At the Qingming Day, people hold memorial ceremonies for deceased family members. So these two festivals are thought to be grave and solemn occasions, and people should wish each other the best of health instead of saying "Happy … Festival". But many Chinese are unsure of what to say, so they just skip the festival greetings.

In addition, people enjoy three public holidays including the New Year's Day, the International Labour Day (May 1) and the National Day (October 1). During these public holidays, you can usually say "happy holiday".

中国重要的传统节日有：春节、元宵节、清明节、端午节、中秋节。这五个传统节日有着不同的文化内涵和习俗，比如春节、元宵节是庆祝新年伊始，中秋节是庆祝全家团圆的，所以这三个节日基本都可以说"×× 节快乐"。端午节是为一位自杀的古代爱国诗人祈福，气氛比较庄重、肃穆，所以有人主张说"端午安康"，不过说"节日快乐"也很常见；

清明节是祭奠逝去的亲人，所以不适合说节日快乐。很多中国人不太确定如何表达，于是就干脆什么都不说了。

另外三个公共节日是元旦、五一劳动节和十一国庆节，简单的一句“节日快乐”就够了。

Xnchūn kuàilè !
新春快乐！

★★★ *Happy New Year!*

Yuánxiāojié kuàilè !
元宵节快乐！

★★★ *Happy Lantern Festival!*

Zhù nǐ quán jiā tuányuán xìngfú !
祝你全家团圆幸福！（春节、中秋节）

★★★ *May you have a happy family reunion!*

Zhù nǐ quán jiā xìngfú měimǎn !
祝你全家幸福美满！（春节、中秋节）

★★★ *May you have a happy and blessed family reunion!*

Zhù nǐ shēntǐ jiànkāng !
祝你身体健康！（端午节）

★★★ *May you be in good health!*

Zhù nǐ Wǔ-Yī /Guóqìng kuàilè !
祝你五一/国庆快乐！

★★★ *Happy Labour/National Day!*

28 How to take a group photo
怎么合影

When taking a group photo, Chinese people usually offer to invite those who are older or who have higher ranks to take the seats at the centre of the frame. An invitee can modestly decline a little and ask someone else to take the seat. When a photo is being taken, Chinese people usually shout "one, two, three, eggplant" so that everyone will smile at the same time, much like saying "one, two, three, cheese" in English.

合影时，中国人一般会主动请职位高、年龄长的人居于中间的重要位置，被邀请的人可以适当谦让一下，请别人站或坐在这里。照的时候，中国人常常会喊“一二三，茄子”，以便大家同时做出微笑的表情。

Nín zuò /zhàn zhèr ba .
您 坐 / 站 这儿吧。

★★★ *Please sit/stand here.*

Nín zěnme néng zuò /zhàn zhèr ?
您怎么能 坐 / 站这儿？

★★★ *How can you sit/stand here?*

Nín yīnggāi zuò /zhàn zài zhōngjiān .
您 应该 坐 / 站 在 中 间 。

★★★ *You should sit/stand in the centre!*

Wǒ jiù zuò /zhàn zài zhèr ba .
我就坐 / 站在这儿吧。

★★★ *Here is fine for me.*

Dàjiā dōu kàn zhèr !
大家都 看这儿！

★★★ *Look here please, everyone!*

Yī èr sān , qiézi !
一二三，茄子！

★★★ *One, two, three, cheese! (In Chinese people say eggplant when taking a photo)*

Zài lái yì zhāng !
再来一 张 ！

★★★ *One more photo!*

29 How to attend a wedding 怎么出席婚礼

At a traditional Chinese wedding, the bride usually dresses in bright red clothing to symbolize joy. To avoid stealing the limelight from the bride, female guests should not wear similar red clothing. Nowadays, many brides choose to wear white wedding dresses. When attending a Chinese wedding, it is very popular to present a red envelop as a gift to convey your blessings. If you would like to give fresh flowers, a bunch of lilies is the best choice. The flower's name sounds like "lifelong happiness and perfect harmony" in Chinese.

Tip: Do not give gifts in odd numbers. Gifts should be given in even numbers to express the wish that good things come in pairs.

中国人的传统婚礼上，新娘一般要穿着红色的衣服，以示喜庆，女客人注意不要穿类似的红衣服，以免和新娘抢风头。现在，新娘穿白色婚纱的也很多。出席中国人的婚礼时，送上一个红包作为祝福，是非常受欢迎的。如果你想送鲜花的话，谐音是"百年好合"的百合是最好的选择。

请注意，送礼物时不要送单数的，双数寄予好事成双的愿望。

Nǐmen zhēn shì lángcái-nǚmào，tiānshēng yí duì！
你们真是郎才女貌，天生一对！

★★★ *You are really a perfect match!*

Zhù nǐmen xīnhūn kuàilè，bǎinián-hǎohé！
祝你们新婚快乐，百年好合！

★★★ *Wish both of you a happy marriage and lifelong happiness and perfect harmony!*

Zhù nǐmen zǎoshēng-guìzǐ，báitóu-dàolǎo！
祝你们早生贵子，白头到老！

★★★ *May you be blessed with children soon and live in conjugal bliss to a ripe old age!*

30 How to visit a patient 怎么看望病人

When visiting patients in China, the most common gifts to bring along are health supplements and fruit (those which the patients can eat). Of course, fresh flowers are also nice. However, you should give neither potted flowers with roots (it implies that the disease has taken root), nor chrysanthemums or azaleas.

When chatting with a patient, you should use those words that are positive, encouraging and comforting. You may also show concern by asking the patient's diet, as the Chinese attach great importance to dietary therapy.

在中国看望病人，最常带的礼物是营养食品和水果（病人可以吃的最好），当然鲜花也不错，但是不要送带根的花（寓意疾病生根的意思），也不要送菊花、杜鹃花。

和病人聊天时多说些正面鼓励、宽慰性的话，也可以关心一下病人的饮食情况，因为中国人很重视食疗的作用。

Hǎohāo xiūxi .
好好休息。

★★★ *Rest well.*

Jīntiān gǎnjué zěnme yàng ?
今天感觉怎么样？

★★★ *How are you feeling today?*

Chīfàn zěnme yàng ?
吃饭怎么样？

★★★ *Are you eating normally?*

Nǐ kàn qǐlai hǎo duō le .
你看起来好多了。

★★★ *You look much better.*

Hǎohāo yǎng bìng , zǎo diǎnr hǎo qǐlai .
好好养病，早点儿好起来。

★★★ *Rest well and get well soon.*

Zhù nín zǎorì kāngfù .
祝您早日康复。

★★★★ *May you have a speedy recovery.*

31 How to react to a bereavement
怎么应对丧事

Do not wear bright colours at a funeral, especially red. Bow to the deceased to express your grief and mourning, and shake hands with relatives and friends to convey your condolences. You may also bring some fresh flowers to serve as a tribute to the deceased.

When we hear from a friend about the death of his/her loved one via email or social media, in addition to showing shock and sorrow, we should console him/her and express our good wishes to the deceased.

出席丧礼时，不要穿颜色鲜艳，尤其是红色的衣服。对逝者鞠躬以示哀悼，和其亲友握手，以示安慰之情。可以带些凭吊用的鲜花。

在通过邮件、社交软件得知对方亲友去世的不幸消息时，除了惊讶和悲痛外，我们一般会对对方进行劝慰，也可以表达对逝者美好的祝福。

Qǐng duō bǎozhòng .
请 多 保 重。

★★★★ *Please take care.*

Bú yào tài shāngxīn le , shēntǐ yàojǐn !
不要太伤心了，身体要紧！

★★★ *Please restrain your grief!*

Zhù lǎorenjia yí lù zǒuhǎo !
祝老人家一路走好！

★★★★ *May the elderly have a smooth final journey (to the nether world)!*

Yuàn tā zài tiāntáng dédào ānxī !
愿他在天堂得到安息！

★★★★ *May the departed rest in heaven!*

Qǐng jié'āi shùnbiàn .
请 节 哀 顺 便。

★★★★★ *May you restrain your grief and be reconciled to the inevitable loss.*

32 How to console someone
怎么安慰别人

When things go wrong for someone, you can show your concern and understanding by consoling them and helping them to divert their attention elsewhere so that they can feel better. This is human nature.

当别人遇到不顺心的事情时，安慰安慰对方，帮助他/她转移注意力，使其心情好受些。这是人之常情。

Pò cái miǎn zāi ba.
破财免灾吧。

★★ *An unexpected loss of money might be a fortune in disguise.*

Méi shénme dàbuliǎo de.
没什么大不了的。

★★ *It is not a big deal.*

Xiǎng kāi diǎnr.
想开点儿。

★★ *Stay optimistic.*

Zài xiǎng yě méi yòng le.
再想也没用了。

★★ *There is no point dwelling on it.*

suàn le, bié xiǎng le.
算了，别想了。

★★ *Forget it. Don't think about it anymore.*

Bié nánguò le!
别难过了！

★★★ *Cheer up!*

Sàiwēng shī mǎ, yān zhī fēi fú.
塞翁失马，焉知非福。

★★★★ *This misfortune may be a blessing in disguise.*

33 How to excuse yourself to go to the toilet
怎么说去卫生间

When excusing yourself to go to the loo, you generally say it in a tactful manner. It is a taboo to use the word cèsuǒ (toilet) or other coarse language, especially in luxurious places where people are dining. The more commonly used words are xǐshǒujiān (washroom) and wèishēngjiān (sanitary room). However, the former is a safer word which is less explicit than the latter.

去卫生间一般要说得委婉一些，尤其是在高档的、吃东西的场合，很忌讳用“厕所”这个词，更

不会直接说某些粗俗的词。“洗手间”和“卫生间”是用得最为普遍的词，相比而言，前者比后者更含蓄，也更安全。

Duì bu qǐ , shīpéi yíhuìr .
对不起，失陪一会儿。

★★★★ *Sorry, please excuse me for a moment.*

Bù hǎoyìsi , wǒ chūqù yíxià .
不好意思，我出去一下。

★★★★ *Sorry, please excuse me for a moment.*

Bù hǎoyìsi , wǒ qù yíxià xíshǒujiān .
不好意思，我去一下洗手间。

★★★★ *Sorry, I'm going to the bathroom.*

Wǒ qù yíxià wèishēngjiān .
我去一下卫生间。

★★★ *I'm going to the bathroom.*

Wǒ qù xǐ yíxià shǒu .
我去洗一下手。

★★★ *I'm going to wash my hands.*

Wǒ qù fāngbiàn yíxià .
我去方便一下。

★ *I'm going to relieve myself.*

Wǒ shàng ge cèsuǒ .
我上个厕所。

★ *I'm going to the toilet.*

34 How to turn someone down
怎么拒绝

To maintain relationships and avoid awkwardness, Chinese people usually refrain from turning someone down directly. They try their best to do this tactfully and sometimes may find an excuse.

Chinese people will not oppose someone directly. They will usually use ambiguous terms such as "likely, maybe, think about it again". Similarly, they do not like to be rejected directly.

为了维护相互间的关系，不让彼此觉得尴尬，中国人一般不会直接拒绝对方，而是尽量委婉一些，有时候还会找些借口。

出于面子，中国人不会直接提出反对，一般说"大概、可能、再考虑考虑"之类模糊的词语；同样，他们也不太喜欢被直接拒绝。

Duìbuqǐ, wǒ lái bu liǎo le.
对不起，我来不了了。

★★★ *Sorry I can't make it.*

Kǒngpà lái bu liǎo.
恐怕来不了。

★★★ *I'm afraid I can't make it.*

Bàoqiàn, kǒngpà bù néng lái.
抱歉，恐怕不能来。

★★★★ *Sorry, I'm afraid I can't make it.*

Wǒ hěn xiǎng lái, kěxī méiyǒu shíjiān.
我很想来，可惜没有时间。

★★★ *I would love to come, but it's a pity I don't have the time.*

Wǒ lái bu liǎo.
我来不了。

★★ *I can't make it.*

Wǒ bù néng lái.
我不能来。

★★ *I cannot come.*

wǒmen zài kǎolǜ kǎolǜ.
我们再考虑考虑。

★★★ *We'll think about it again.*

Kěyǐ zài shāngliang.
可以再商量。

★★★ *(We) can discuss this again.*

Kǒngpà zhèyàng bù xíng.
恐怕这样不行。

★★★ *I'm afraid this does not work.*

Wǒ juéde yǒu wèntí.
我觉得有问题。

★★★ *I think there's a problem.*

Wǒ bú tài tóngyì.
我不太同意。

★★★★ *I don't quite agree.*

Wǒ bù kěyǐ lái.
● 我不可以来。

I am forbidden from coming.

35 How to make suggestions 怎么提出建议

When making suggestions, you need to do this tactfully so that people will not feel pressured or being commanded.

Beginners in Chinese like to use the word "yīnggāi (should)" when making suggestions, however this gives

people the feeling that you are imposing your views on them. Therefore, it is better to use "it is best to" instead.

提建议的时候也尽量委婉一些，避免让对方觉得有压力，或者有被命令的感觉。

初学中文的朋友喜欢用"应该"来提建议，其实这个词会给人一种强加于人的感觉，用"最好"这个词就好多了。

Qǐng duō tí bǎoguì yìjiàn !
请多提宝贵意见！

★★★★ *Please feel free to make any suggestions!*

Qǐng duōduō zhǐjiào !
请多多指教！

★★★★ *Please give me your advice!*

Jìngqǐng cìjiào !
敬请赐教！

★★★★★ *Please enlighten me with your advice!*

Nín yǒu shénme yìjiàn , qǐng jǐnguǎn tí .
您有什么意见，请尽管提。

★★★★ *Put forward all your opinions please.*

húanyíng duì zhè ge wèntí chàngsǔoyùyán .
欢迎对这个问题畅所预言。

★★★ *You are welcome to speak openly about this problem.*

Jiǔ diǎn kěyǐ kāishǐ ma ?
九点可以开始吗？

★★★ *Can it start at nine o'clock?*

Jiǔ diǎn kāishǐ zěnme yàng ?
九点开始怎么样？

★★★ *How about starting at nine o'clock?*

Wǒ jiànyì jiǔ diǎn kāishǐ .
我建议九点开始。

★★★★ *I suggest starting at nine o'clock.*

Jiǔ diǎn kāishǐ ba ?
九点开始吧？

★★ *Shall we start at nine o'clock?*

Zuìhǎo jiǔ diǎn kāishǐ .
最好九点开始。

★★ *It is best to start at nine o'clock.*

Xīwàng nénggòu jiǔ diǎn kāishǐ .
希望能够九点开始。

★★★ *We wish you to start at nine o'clock.*

Nǐ yīnggāi jiǔ diǎn kāishǐ .
你应该九点开始。

★ *You should start at nine o'clock.*

36 How to say and respond to thanks
怎么感谢及回应

When thanking someone, you can either press your palms together near your chest and nod at the same time, or bow slightly to convey your appreciation. If they have given you substantial help, it is reasonable to give them a suitable gift.

When responding to thanks from someone, you should downplay the help you have provided. You

should say that it's no big deal, and get them to dispense with pleasantries.

感谢的时候可以双手合十放在胸前，同时点头示意；也可以稍稍鞠个躬来表达。如果对方给了你比较大的帮助，送个合适的礼物来感谢也是符合情理的。

回答感谢时，可以淡化自己所帮的忙，要表达出这是小事一桩，并让对方不要那么客气。

Duō xiè !
多 谢！

★★★ *Thank you very much!*

Duō xiè nǐ le !
多 谢 你 了！

★★★ *Thank you very much!*

Biǎoshì gǎnxiè !
表 示 感 谢！

★★★ *I'd like to express my thanks!*

Gěi nín tiān máfan le !
给 您 添 麻 烦 了！

★★★ *(Sorry to) trouble you!*

Ràng nín fèixīn le !
让 您 费 心 了！

★★★★ *Sorry for troubling you so much!*

Bù zhīdào gāi zěnme gǎnxiè cái hǎo !
不 知 道 该 怎 么 感 谢 才 好！

★★★ *Words cannot express my thanks to you!*

Búshèng gǎnjī !
不胜感激！

★★★★★ *Thank you very much!*

Méi shénme de .
没什么的。

★★★ *It's nothing.*

Xiǎo shìr .
小事儿。

★★★ *It's no big deal.*

Bú yòng xiè .
不用谢。

★★★ *You're welcome.*

Bié kèqi .
别客气。

★★★ *You're welcome. / No worries.*

Nǐ tài kèqi le .
你太客气了。

★★★ *You're too kind.*

Xiè / kèqi shénme a !
谢 / 客气什么啊！

★★ *You don't have to (thank me/be so polite)!*

37 How to preside over a meeting
怎么主持会议

On formal occasions, guests should be mentioned in order of their ranks from high to low in the introductory remarks. This is similar to opening speeches in English.

Tip: Do not start your speech with "hello, all" as it sounds abrupt and impolite. When speaking, it is best

not to use "you (all)" as the audience will not be able to connect with you. It is best to use "everybody" and "everyone".

和英语一样，在正式场合，开场白一般都是以职位的高低依次提到在场的嘉宾并问候。

请注意：开场白的时候不要直接说"你们好"，这样说显得既突兀又没有礼貌；中间也最好不要说"你们"，因为这个词显得和听众有距离，最好说"大家""各位"。

Dàjiā hǎo!
大家好！

★★ *Hello, everybody!*

Zūnjìng de Wáng júzhǎng, gè wèi láibīn,
尊敬的王局长，各位来宾，
péngyoumen, wǎnshang hǎo!
朋友们，晚上好！

★★★★★ *Distinguished Director-General Wang, guests, friends, good evening!*

Wǒmen hěn róngxìng de yāoqǐng dàole Chén huìzhǎng.
我们很荣幸地邀请到了陈会长。

★★★★ *We are honoured to have President Chen with us today.*

Xiànzài yǒuqǐng Chén huìzhǎng .
现在有请 陈 会 长。

★★★★ *President Chen, please.*

Xiàmiàn qǐng Wáng júzhǎng jiǎnghuà !
下面 请 王 局长 讲话！

★★★ *Next, let us invite Director-General Wang to take the floor.*

Zhǎngshēng yǒuqǐng !
掌 声 有请！

★★★★ *A round of applause please!*

Qǐng dàjiā yǐ rèliè de zhǎngshēng huānyíng
请大家以热烈的 掌 声 欢 迎
Wáng júzhǎng !
王 局长！

★★★★ *Please give a warm round of applause to welcome Director-General Wang!*

Gǎnxiè Wáng júzhǎng de jīngcǎi fāyán !
感谢 王 局长的精彩发言！

★★★ *Thank you Director-General Wang for the captivating speech!*

Nǐmen hǎo !
● 你们 好！

Hello, all of you.

38 How to complain and apologise 怎么抱怨和道歉

Face is important to Chinese people, so they generally do not express dissatisfaction or lodge complaints directly. They expect other people also act this way, to avoid awkwardness or even unhappiness. It is proper to complain in a more tactful manner.

When apologising, you can nod and bow slightly, or bow with your hands folded before you. If you have caused

somc damagc to someone, you can present a suitable gift to express your sincerity in apologising to them.

因为注重面子，所以中国人一般不会直接表达不满或者抱怨，同样也不喜欢对方这样做，否则会比较尴尬，甚至很不愉快。建议用比较委婉的方式。

道歉的时候可以微微点头鞠躬，也可以行一个抱拳礼。如果给对方造成了一定的伤害，还可以送上一份合适的礼物，以表达自己真诚的歉意。

Zhè ge cài tài xián le !
这个菜太咸了！

★★ *This dish is too salty!*

Zhè ge cài xiánsǐ le !
这个菜咸死了！

★★ *This dish is nothing but salty!*

Zhè ge cài yě tài xián le ba ?
这个菜也太咸了吧？

★★ *Isn't this dish too salty!*

Zhè ge cài yǒu diǎnr xián le !
这个菜有点儿咸了！

★★★ *This dish is a little salty!*

Kěyǐ kuài diǎnr ma ?
可以快点儿吗？

★★ *Can you please hurry up?*

Nǐmen néng bu néng kuài diǎnr ?
你们能不能快点儿？

★ *Can you please hurry up?*

Nǐmen zěnme zhème màn ?
你们怎么这么慢？

★ *Why do you serve food so late?*

Duìbuqǐ ! Qǐng nǐ yuánliàng !
对不起！请你原谅！

★★★ *Sorry! I beg your pardon!*

Xiàng nǐ dàoqiàn !
向你道歉！

★★★ *I'm sorry!*

Zhēn bù hǎoyìsi / duìbuqǐ !
真不好意思/对不起！

★★★ *I'm very sorry!*

Zhēn de hěn bàoqiàn !
真的很抱歉！

★★★ *I'm really sorry!*

Xiàng nǐ biǎoshì qiànyì !
向你表示歉意！

★★★ *I'd like to express my apology to you!*

Qǐng duō bāohán !
请多包涵！

★★★★ *Please forgive me!*

Qǐng jiēshòu wǒ de qiànyì !
请接受我的歉意！

★★★★ *Please accept my apology!*

39 How to entreat and forbid
怎么请求和禁止

Use terms of respect when asking someone for help. To make your request come across more strongly, you can bow with your hands folded before you.

There are varying degrees to forbid the actions of others. You should use words appropriate to the situation.

请求别人帮忙的时候要用一些客气的敬辞，如

果想加强一下请求的程度，也可以行一下抱拳礼。

禁止的程度有高有低，应该根据场合选择适当的词语。

Bàituō le !
拜托了！

★★★ *Please!*

Máfan nǐ bāng wǒ yíxià .
麻烦你帮我一下。

★★★ *May I trouble you to help me?*

Bàituō nǐ bāng wǒ yíxià .
拜托你帮我一下。

★★★★ *Please, may I trouble you to help me?*

Yǒu jiàn shì xiǎng má fán nín yíxià !
有件事想麻烦您一下！

★★★★ *I have something that may need your help.*

Wǒ xiǎng qiú nǐ yí jiàn shì .
我想求你一件事。

★★★ *I have to seek your help for one thing.*

Màomèi wèn yíxià ...
冒昧问一下……

★★★★ *Pardon my asking...*

Láojià ...
劳驾……

★★★★ *Excuse me, may I trouble you to...(do something)*

Qǐng bú yào chídào !
请不要迟到！

★★★ *Please don't be late!*

Bù zhǔn chídào !
不准迟到！

★★★ *(You) must not be late!*

Xièjué cānguān !
谢绝参观！

★★★★ *No visitors allowed!*

Jìnzhǐ pāizhào !
禁止拍照！

★★★ *No photography!*

Qǐng wù pāizhào !
请勿拍照！

★★★★ *Please don't take photos!*

Duìbuqǐ , zhèli bù néng pāizhào !
对不起，这里不能拍照！

★★★ *Sorry, photo-taking is not allowed here!*

40 How to chat with Chinese people
怎么和中国人聊天

It is rather relaxing to chat with a Chinese; you do not have to worry much about taboos. Under normal circumstances, you can ask questions about their age, their job, where do they come from, how many children do they have, and so on. At times, it is fine even if you ask them about their salary.

Some questions such as asking about the age may seem personal to Westerners, but not to the elderly

Chinese people. They welcome such questions, which they consider as people's concern about and interest in their health.

和中国人聊天是比较轻松的，你不用担心那么多的禁忌。一般情况下，你可以问对方多大、做什么工作、从哪里来、有几个孩子，等等，有时候问一下他们的收入也不是大的问题。

有些对西方人来说属于隐私的问题，比如年龄，对中国的老年人来说却常常很受欢迎，因为在他们看来这是对他们的健康感兴趣。

Nǐ zài nǎr gōngzuò?
你在哪儿工作？

★★★ *Where do you work?*

Nǐ zuò shénme gōngzuò?
你做什么工作？

★★★ *What do you do?*

Nǐ jiā shì nǎr / nǎli de?
你家是哪儿/哪里的？

★★★ *Where is your hometown?*

Nǐ shì Zhōngguó nǎr / nǎli de?
你是中国哪儿/哪里的？

★★★ *Which part of China do you come from?*

Nǐ jīnnián duō dà ?
你今年 多大？

★★★ *How old are you?*

Nǐ yǒu háizi ma ?
你有孩子吗？

★★★ *Do you have any children?*

Nǐ yǒu jǐ ge háizi ?
你有几个孩子？

★★★ *How many children do you have?*

Nǐ de gōngzī hěn gāo ba ?
你的工资 很 高吧？

★★ *Your salary must be high, right?*

Nǐ píngshí yǒu xiē shénme àihào ?
你平时有些什么爱好？

★★★ *What is your hobby in your free time?*

Nǐ zhōumò yìbān zuò shénme ?
你周末一般做什么？

★★★ *What do you usually do at the weekend?*

Nǐmen nàr tiānqì zěnme yàng ?
你们那儿天气怎么 样？

★★★ *What is the weather like in your locality?*

TWO

ACTING WITH MANNERS

The concept of Chinese etiquette is not only reflected in their language, but also in their behaviours. The basic principle of behaviours is the same as speaking: behave modestly, put others before oneself, respect others and even elevate their status.

In addition, Chinese have a deep-rooted traditional idea: pursue happiness while avoiding misfortune. This can also be found in their language. They would not refer to something inauspicious directly, and would even avoid using their homophones which might invite negative associations.

做得有礼

中国文化中的礼仪观念不但反映在语言上，更反映在行为上。行为举止的基本原则和说话一样，也是谦恭待人，先人后己，尊重甚至抬高对方。

此外，中国人有着根深蒂固的传统思想，即趋福避祸，因此在生活中喜欢使用谐音的手法。不好的事情中国人不但不直接说出来，甚至连和它们谐音的词语也会因引起不好的联想而尽量避免使用。

01 Why gift-giving is a must
为什么总要送礼物

Gift-giving is very important to the Chinese. Be it festivals, birthdays, weddings, first meetings, sending off guests, expressing gratitude or apologies, visiting other people or celebrations, they always express affection and enhance relationships through gifts. As the Chinese saying goes, "The gift is trifling, but the feeling is profound," meaning it does not matter if the gift is inexpensive, for it is the thought behind it that counts. There is another Chinese saying, "It is impolite not to reciprocate," meaning it is disrespectful not to offer a

gift in return after receiving one.

送礼对于中国人来说是件非常重要的事情，无论是过节假日、过生日、参加婚礼，还是刚见面、告别，无论是感谢、道歉，还是看望、庆祝，他们都喜欢通过礼物来传递和增进感情。中国有句俗话叫“礼轻情意重”，意思是礼物贵不贵重不是最重要的，重要的是送礼人的情意；中国人还有句俗话叫“来而不往非礼也”，意思是说，收到礼物而不回赠对方，是种失礼的行为。

Sòng nǐ yí ge Zhōngguójié， zhù nǐ de rìzi
送你一个中国结，祝你的日子
hónghónghuǒhuǒ！
红红火火！

★★★ *May this Chinese knot bring you a prosperous life!*

Zhè shì wǒ zìjǐ zuò de jiǎnzhǐ， xīwàng nǐ xǐhuan.
这是我自己做的剪纸，希望你喜欢。

★★★ *I made this paper-cuting myself. I hope you like it!*

An old saying

lǐshàng-wǎnglái
礼尚往来

It is appreciated to return politeness for politeness.

02 What not to give
哪些礼物不能送

Owing to their traditional thought of pursuing happiness and avoiding misfortune, Chinese people consider what is associated with something bad as a taboo. For example, they do not give watches or clocks to the elderly people as sòng zhōng (giving a clock) sounds like sòng zhōng (burying a deceased elder in the family). They do not give umbrellas or pears to lovers or friends as sǎn (umbrella) sounds similar to sàn (break-up) while lí (pear) sounds similar to lí (separate). They do not give chrysanthemums which are usually used as offerings to the deceased. They do not give shoes to non-family members as xié (shoes) sounds like xié (evil). They do not give medicine to people who are in good health. In addition, quantity and colour play a role in the selection of gifts. For example, Chinese people generally like even numbers and dislike odd numbers, because even numbers symbolize auspiciousness and good luck, therefore wedding gifts in particular should be in pairs. A Chinese does not give a green hat to a man as this is a metaphor suggesting he has an unfaithful wife. Chinese people do not wrap gifts in black or white, as those are the colours used in funerals.

趋福避祸的传统思想让中国人对那些可能引起不好联想的事物有所忌讳，比如：送礼物时，不给长者送表或钟，因为“送钟”谐音“送终”；不给情人或朋友送“伞”和“梨”，因为“伞”谐音“散”，“梨”谐音“离”；不给家人以外的人送鞋，因为“鞋”谐音“邪”。人们也不会送菊花，因为那是送给逝者的；不给健康的人送药，因为有带去疾病的不好联想。另外，挑选礼物对数量、颜色也有一定的选择，比

如中国人一般喜欢双数，不太喜欢单数，因为双数象征吉祥和好运，尤其是结婚的礼物往往要送一对，取“好事成双”之意。在颜色方面，中国偏爱红色。如果你给男士送一顶绿色帽子，这暗喻他有一个不忠的妻子。生活中少用黑、白色作为包装，因为这是丧礼用的颜色。

Nǐ yào hé wǒ fēnlí (lí) ma??
你要和我分离（梨）吗？

★★★ *Do you want to split up with me? (In Chinese the word for pear sounds the same as the word for leave. If you split a pear with someone, it can also mean that you want to leave them.)*

Yào sòng jiù sòng yí duì ba .
要送就送一对吧。

★★★ *Just give it in pairs!*

An old saying

Guài rén bù zhī lǐ , zhī lǐ bú guài rén .
怪人不知礼，知礼不怪人。

You won't blame other people if you are educated and well-balanced; vice versa.

03 What to give 送什么礼物好

The first thing to consider when giving a gift is the relationship between yourself and the recipient. Then you take their age, occupation, personality, hobbies, and so on into consideration. Generally speaking, young people prefer gifts that are fashionable, dynamic and distinctive, such as cosmetics, sporting products, and so on. Middle-aged Chinese prefer gifts that are practical, tasteful and beneficial to health, for example, electronic products, clothing, and so on. However, the elderly people prefer gifts that take their health and other specific needs into consideration, for example, health products.

Of course, red envelops are popular festive gifts. It is welcome to give red envelops to children on their birthdays or in the New Year.

送礼时首先要考虑自己和对方之间的关系，然后还要考虑对方的年龄、职业、性格、爱好等。一般来说，年轻人喜欢的礼物是时尚、动感、与众不同的，比如化妆品、运动用品等；中年人喜欢的礼物是实用的、有品位的、兼顾健康的，比如电子产品、服饰等；而老年人喜欢的礼物是健康的、体贴的、针对性强的，首选的就是保健品。

当然喽，红包也是个很有喜庆特色的礼物，过年过节、或过生日时，给未成年人一个红包都是很受欢迎的。

Hē diǎnr pǔ'ěr chá duì wèi yǒu hǎochu .
喝点儿普洱茶对胃有好处。

★★★ *It is good for your stomach to have some Pu'er tea.*

Tā xǐhuan lánsè , zhè ge shìhé tā .
他喜欢蓝色，这个适合他。

★★★ *He likes blue, this suits his taste.*

Zài wǎng shang mǎi ba , kěyǐ zhíjiē jì dào tā shǒu li .
在网上买吧，可以直接寄到他手里。

★★★ *Buy the gift online, and it can be delivered directly to him.*

An old saying

Qiān lǐ sòng émáo , lǐ qīng qíngyì zhòng .
千里送鹅毛，礼轻情意重。

Goose feather sent from afar, light as it is, is a token of rofound friendship.

04 How to serve tea
怎么倒茶

Tea is a drink commonly served by Chinese people to their guests. When pouring tea for your guests, you should ensure that the cup is not filled to the brim. It is best to fill it to 70 percent full as this makes it easier for your guests to take the cup without scalding their hands. When someone pours tea for you, you may extend your hand as a gesture for "please", or you may bend your fingers and gently tap the table to express your gratitude to them.

As a sign of respect, you should serve and receive tea with both hands.

中国人招待客人的常用饮品就是茶。在给客人

倒茶的时候，注意不要太满，七分满最好，否则因为烫手，客人不容易接，有冒犯之意。这个时候，客人可以伸出一只手做出“请”的意思，或者用手指轻轻地叩打桌面，以示对倒茶人的谢意。

为表示尊敬，递茶的人要用双手，接茶的人也要用双手。

Nǐ xǐhuan hē lǜchá háishi hóngchá ?
你喜欢喝绿茶还是红茶？

★★★ *Do you like green tea or black tea?*

Chángchang zhè ge chá zěnme yàng .
尝尝这个茶怎么样。

★★★ *How about trying some of this tea?*

Huàn bēi chá ba ?
换杯茶吧？

★★★ *What about changing to another type of tea?*

An old saying

Dài kè chá wéi xiān , chá hǎo kè cháng lái .
待客茶为先，茶好客常来。

Tea comes first to treat guests and good tea can draw frequent guests.

05 How to take a seat
怎么就座

Seating arrangements reflect differences in status, ranks and ages among people, thus guests must not be seated randomly. The seating protocol is as follows: a host will invite the principal senior guest to sit at the most important seat, which usually faces the main entrance of the room, from where it is easy to see what is happening in the room. When invited to do so, the principal guest can modestly decline a little and ask the host to sit there. After the main guest sits down, the host will sit at his/her side and invite other guests to sit around them.

Generally speaking, the seat near the exit is least important, but if you keep a low profile and are delighted to serve other people, it is praiseworthy for you to help pass on the dishes from here.

When eating or drinking, you should lean to the table as closely as possible. Otherwise, you can lean back away from the table. Upon the arrival of an important guest, you should stand up immediately to salute him/her.

座位反映了人们之间的身份或职位高低、年龄长幼，所以不要轻意乱坐。入坐时，主人会请重要的、年长的客人坐在最重要的位置。这个位置一般正对着房间的主要出口，以方便他了解整个房间的情况。主客适当地和主人谦让，落座后，主人陪坐在旁边，同时会礼貌地邀请其他客人坐在自己和主客两侧的位置。

一般来说，靠近出口的座位是重要性较低的位置。不过如果你很低调，并且乐于服务别人，坐在这个位置帮忙接一下菜也是很让人赞许的。

用餐时人的身体要尽量靠近餐桌；没有用餐时，身体可以适当靠后。有重要客人时，应该立刻起身致意。

Nín yīnggāi zuò zhèr !
您 应该 坐这儿！

★★★★ *Please do sit here!*

Zuò zhèr yě yíyàng !
坐 这儿也一样！

★★★ *I can sit here, too.*

Bié tài jiǎngjiu le , suíbiàn zuò ba .
别太讲究了，随便 坐吧。

★★★ *Don't be polite, just sit wherever you want.*

An old saying

Gōngjìng bùrú cóngmìng !
恭敬不如从命！

It is better to accept the arrangement deferentially than to decline it courteously.

06 How to hold and place chopsticks
怎么拿放筷子

Chopsticks are an indispensable tool in Chinese dining; therefore they have been endowed with many cultural connotations in the long history of their use. For example, it is inauspicious to place your chopsticks unevenly on the table or to stick chopsticks upright in a rice bowl. This may make others associate them with a funeral. Tapping the bowl with your chopsticks may produce the image of a beggar; using the wrong ends of the chopsticks to pick up food may make other people think you are too eager for food; while picking up the chopsticks, pointing your index finger or your chopsticks at someone implies an accusation; and sucking your chopsticks is also considered an impolite behaviour.

Tip: As a guest, wait until the hosts pick up their chopsticks and invite everyone to start eating before picking up yours.

筷子是中国人必不可少的用餐工具，因此在长期的使用中也被赋予了许多文化涵义。比如，把筷子长短不齐地放在桌子上，或者把筷子竖插在米饭中，都是不吉利的，这会让人和丧事联系起来。用筷子敲碗，会让人联想起乞丐。把筷子颠倒使用，给人一种饥不择食的感觉。举着筷子伸出食指，或者用筷子指着人，都会有指责他人之意。还有，把筷子含在嘴里吸吮，也是种很不得体的行为。

请注意：客人要在主人拿起筷子请大家开始吃时，客人才好动筷。

Nǐ huì yòng kuàizi ma ?
你会 用 筷子吗？

★★★ *Can you use chopsticks?*

Kuàizi búyào ná dī le .
筷子不要拿低了。

★★★ *Don't hold the chopsticks at the bottom part.*

liǎng zhī kuàizi yào náqí .
两只筷子要拿齐。

★★★ *Hold the chopsticks evenly.*

Wǒ jiā bu qǐlái .
我夹不起来。

★★★ *I can't pick it up.*

An old saying

sāncháng-liǎng duǎn
三 长 两 短

It signifies death to place chopsticks unevenly on the table since a coffin is made up of three long and two short plates.

07 How to use chopsticks to pick up food 怎么用筷子取菜

A typical Chinese dining setting consists of a round table with a Lazy Susan placed in the centre. To avoid being rude, before spinning the Lazy Susan, you must observe if someone is serving themselves or is about to serve themselves. If communal chopsticks are provided, you should use them to select food. Take only one serving each time instead of multiple servings. When a dish is served, do not take it immediately. Wait for the host to urge you to eat before taking it. Also, do not reach across another person with your chopsticks to pick up food. Do not dig around or pick through the food with your chopsticks.

When you see that someone cannot reach food, you can take the initiative to serve them with the use of the communal chopsticks. When transferring the food, you should also use your bowl and plate to catch any drips.

中餐一般都用带有转盘的圆桌，所以在转转盘时一定要注意是否有人正在或将要取菜，否则会显得失礼。取菜时有公筷的话要用公筷；每次只取一

次的量，而不要连续取多次；不要刚上一道菜就马上去取，要等主人劝吃再去取。也不要越过别人的筷子取菜，更不要用筷子在菜盘里来回翻找。

当你看到有人够不着菜时，你可以主动用公筷帮他取菜。取菜时，要用自己的碗碟去迎接，不要把菜或汤汁洒落在别的菜里面。

Fúwùyuán, qǐng ná yì shuāng gōngkuài.
服务员，请拿一双公筷。

★★★ *Waiter/Waitress, please give us a pair of communal chopsticks.*

Zhè ge cài nǐ gòu de zháo ma?
这个菜你够得着吗？

★★★ *Can you reach this dish?*

Lái chángchang zhè ge cài.
来尝尝这个菜。

★★★ *Come, try this dish!*

Bié kèqi, wǒ zìjǐ lái.
别客气，我自己来。

★★★ *No need to be ploite. I can reach it.*

An old saying

Chīzhe wǎn li de, kànzhe guō li de.
吃着碗里的，看着锅里的。

Eating the food from one's bowl while keeping an eye on the pot (implying the person is very greedy)

08 How to speak with numbers
怎么玩转数字

Numbers often carry significant meanings for Chinese people. This significance may be well beyond your imagination. There are two reasons why numbers are special. First, some numbers have certain significance in the culture and history of China. Second, Chinese people like to accord additional meanings to numbers by making use of homophony.

8 (bā) is the favourite number of Chinese people, because it signifies prosperity and sounds similar to fā(prosper). They also like the number 6 (liù), which has a similar sound as lù (road). When 6 is paired with 8, the number combination can mean every road is prosperous. Therefore, combinations such as 168 (be prosperous all the way), 668, 888, 918 (going to be prosperous right away) are very popular. They do not like the number 4 (sì) as it sounds like sǐ (death). Therefore, number combinations such as 14, 44, 444, 154, 514 are detested.

Chinese netizens have proven the significance of numbers in Chinese by creating a crazy festival just because the number 1 implies a single man or woman:

Singles Day, on November 11. The four 1s in the date resemble four sticks lined together to symbolize numerous single men and women. On this day every year, online sales volume easily amounts to tens of billions of Renminbi yuan.

数字对中国人来说，它的意义可能远远超出你的想象。数字之所以特殊，一是由于中国历史文化方面的原因，二是中国人喜欢运用谐音而赋予了它们更多的含义。

中国人最喜欢的数字是8，因为它和表示发财、发达的“发”谐音；中国人也很喜欢与“路”谐音的6，因为6在和8的数字组合中可以表示每条路都发达，所以像168, 668, 888,918这些数字都很受欢迎。

中国人不喜欢4，因为它和“死”谐音，所以像14，44，444，154，514这样的数字不被中国人喜欢。

中国的网民还仅仅因为数字1的形状，就创造了一个节日——“双十一”光棍节。11月11日，像四个棍子的1连续排列，用来比喻单身的光棍。现在“双十一”又多了一层含义，就是“双十一网购狂欢节”，每年的这一天，网上的销售额轻易就达到数百亿元。

Nǐ de shǒujī hào zhēn niú, yào fā yào fā yào fā a
你的手机号真牛，要发要发要发啊
yāo bā yāo bā yāo bā!
（1 8 1 8 1 8）！

★★★ *Your mobile phone number is so cool; you are going to be prosperous all the time!*

Sòng nǐ shíyī duǒ méigui, dàibiǎo wǒ duì nǐ
送你11朵玫瑰，代表我对你
yìxīn-yíyì.
一心一意。

★★★ *Here are 11 roses to represent my heart and love for you.*

An old saying

Yào xiǎng fā, bù lí bā.
要想发，不离八。

Never forget 8 if you want to be prosperous.

数字含义

Meanings of Numbers

yī liù bā： yí lù fā
168：一路发

be prosperous all the way

liù liù bā： lù lù fā
668：路路发

be prosperous in every way

bā bā bā： fā fā fā
888：发发发

be always prosperous

jiǔ yāo bā： jiù yào fā
918：就要发

going to be prosperous right away

yāo sì： yào sǐ
14：要死

going to die

sì sì sì： sǐ sǐ sǐ
444：死死死

die die die

yāo wǔ sì： yào wǒ sǐ
154：要我死

want me (to) die

wǔ yāo sì： wǒ yào sǐ
514：我要死

I am going to die

wǔ èr líng : wǒ ài nǐ
520：我爱你

I love you

yī sān yī sì : yìshēng-yíshì
1314：一生一世

one's whole life

wǔ èr líng yī sān yī sì : wǒ ài nǐ yìshēng-yíshì
5201314：我爱你一生一世

I love you all my life

wǔ wǔ wǔ wū wū wū
555：呜呜呜

sobbing

bā bā liù : báibái lou
886：拜拜喽

bye for now

09 How to write an email
怎么写邮件

The difference between written and spoken Chinese languages is rather significant. Written language is used in emails; therefore the words and tone used are generally more polite and respectful than spoken language. Special attention should be paid to using the correct terms of address and signature as it directly reflects the relationship between you and the recipient.

It is quite impolite and disrespectful to address the recipient by last name, given name or full name unless you are very familiar. The correct way is to use "surname + title". As for the signature, the safe and formal way is to use your full name, which is a sign of respect to the recipient with a higher rank and a sign of modesty to one with a lower rank. If the recipient is someone whom you are familiar with, you can also use your given name (with the exception of a mono-syllable given name).

中文有口语和书面语之分，区别是比较大的。写邮件即属于书面语，语气和用词一般都比口语客气、委婉，特别是在称呼对方和最后署名时尤其要注意方式，因为这直接体现了你和收信人之间的关系。

在邮件中，直接称呼姓、名和全名都是相当不礼貌、不尊重对方的做法，正确的做法是用“姓+头衔”来称呼；署名可以分情况，保险而正式的做法是写上自己的全名，这对资历比自己高的人来说，是尊重对方的体现；对资历比自己低的人来说，则是谦虚的体现。当然如果双方非常熟悉的话，也可以只用自己的名（单名除外）。

Lǐ lǎoshī, nín hǎo!
李老师，您好！

★★★★ *Hello, Mr/Miss/Mrs Li!*

Zhù nín zhōumò kuàilè!
祝您周末快乐！

★★★★ *Wishing you a pleasant weekend!*

Cǐzhì jìnglǐ.
此致敬礼。

★★★★ *Yours respectfully.*

Dàwěi, nǐ hǎo!
大伟，你好！

★★★ *Hello, Dawei!*

Hěn gāoxìng shōudào nǐ de láixìn!
很高兴收到你的来信！

★★★ *I am very pleased to hear from you!*

Hěn jiǔ méiyǒu nǐ de xiāoxi, hái hǎo ma?
很久没有你的消息，还好吗？

★★★ *I haven't heard from you for a long time, how are you?*

Zhù nǐ zài Zhōngguó yíqiè shùnlì!
祝你在中国一切顺利！

★★★ *I hope that all goes well with you in China!*

Zhù nǐ xuéxí jìnbù!
祝你学习进步！

★★★ *Wishing that you make great progress in your study!*

Zūnjìng de Chén huìzhǎng， nínhǎo ！
尊敬的陈会长，您好！

★★★★ *How do you do, respected President Chen!*

Fēicháng gǎnxiè nín bǎimáng zhī zhōng chōukòng huíxìn ！
非常感谢您百忙之中抽空回信！

★★★★ *Many thanks for taking the time off your busy schedule to reply!*

Jìngzhù shēntǐ jiànkāng ！
敬祝身体健康！

★★★★ *I wish you good health!*

An old saying

Jìng rén zhě， rén héng jìng zhī .
敬人者，人恒敬之。

Those who respect other people will be always respected by other people.

10 How to choose a good Chinese name
怎么起个好的中文名字

As Confucius said, when things are not addressed by their proper names, one's argument cannot stand to reason, and when one's argument does not stand to reason, nothing can be accomplished. Therefore, a good Chinese name should not only sound catchy and melodious, it should also carry good meanings, allowing other people to remember you easily. A very good example of this is Coca-Cola. Among all the foreign brands in China, its Chinese name is not only homonymous and melodious, but also meaningful! Coca is transliterated as kěkǒu, which means tasty, while Cola is transliterated as kělè, which means joyful. Combined together, they become an unforgettable brand name when heard.

A name should neither be chosen arbitrarily nor be a mere transliteration of your English name. When choosing a name, avoid using homophones of words with negative meanings, so as to prevent people from associating your name with something bad.

The commonly used way of choosing a Chinese

name is to first pick one syllable from your surname, and either one or two syllables from your given name. Find the Chinese words which carry good meanings and which sound like the chosen syllables.

孔子说，名不正则言不顺，言不顺则事不成，意思是一个人名分不对的话，那么他的言语就没有说服力，就做不成事。一个好的中文名字不但说起来朗朗上口，听起来清楚悦耳，而且具有美好的寓意，让人很快就记住你。一个非常好的例子就是“可口可乐”，恐怕没有哪个外国品牌的名字能像它这么既谐音，又动听，而且意义非常棒！Coca 用“可口（tasty）”来指代，Cola 用“可乐（joyful）”来指代，合起来造就了一个令人过耳不忘的品牌形象。

好的中文名字不是随便起的，也不是英语名字的简单语音转换。还要注意不能和意义不太好的词语谐音，以免产生不好的联想。

常用的方法是：从英语名字的姓和名里面分别找出和汉语拼音相似的音节，姓里面取一个，名里面取一个或两个，然后根据音节含义较好的意思，选出汉字。

中文名字举例

Examples of Chinese Names

Simon (given name) —— Sī (to think) míng (bright) ——思明

Reed (family name) —— Lǐ (one of the most common family names) ——李

Simon Reed —— Lǐ Sīmíng——李思明

Tip: Simon Reed is a lawyer.

Srila (given name)—— Sī (to think) ruì (wise) ——思睿

Kurup (family name) —— Gù (one of the most common family names) ——顾

Srila Kurup —— Gù Sīruì —— 顾思睿

Tip: Sirla Kurup is a teacher.

Shuí gěi nǐ qǐ de míngzi ? Zhēn hǎotīng !
谁给你起的名字？ 真 好听！

★★★ *Who gave you such a nice name?*

Nǐ de míngzi qǐ de zhēn hǎo !
你的名字起得真 好！

★★★ *Your name is great!*

Nǐ de míngzi zhēn xiǎngliàng !
你的名字 真 响 亮 ！

★★★ *Your name sounds great!*

Zǎojiù tīngshuōguò nǐ de míngzi le !
早就 听说过你的名字了！

★★★★ *I heard your name a long time ago!*

An old saying

Míng bú zhèng , yán bú shùn .
名不正，言不顺。

When things are not addressed by their proper names, one's argument cannot stand to reason.

责任编辑：翟淑蓉
英文编辑：卢　敏
封面设计：厚　冬
责任印制：汪　洋

图书在版编目（CIP）数据

彬彬有礼 ：实用中文交际指南 ：汉、英 / 余成功著. -- 北京 ：华语教学出版社，2018.6
ISBN 978-7-5138-1577-2

Ⅰ. ①彬… Ⅱ. ①余… Ⅲ. ①礼仪—汉语—对外汉语教学—教学参考资料 Ⅳ. ① H195.4

中国版本图书馆 CIP 数据核字（2018）第 104261 号

彬彬有礼——中文交际实用指南

余成功　著

*

©华语教学出版社有限责任公司

华语教学出版社有限责任公司出版
（中国北京百万庄大街24号　邮政编码 100037）
电话：(86)10-68320585　68997826
传真：(86)10-68997826　68326333
网址：www.sinolingua.com.cn
电子信箱：hyjx@sinolingua.com.cn
北京玺诚印务有限公司印刷
2018年（32开）第1版
2018年第1版第1次印刷
（汉英）
ISBN 978-7-5138-1577-2
定价：29.00元